the

VIRTUES
OF HOLINESS

the

VIRTUES
OF HOLINESS

The Basics of Spiritual Struggle

Juan Luis Lorda

Scepter

This edition published in June 2010 by
Scepter Publishers, Inc.
P.O. Box 211, New York, N.Y. 10018
www.scepterpublishers.org

English translation by Bernard Browne.

Composition, cover, and text design by Rose Design

Printed in the United States of America

ISBN-13: 978-1-59417-090-4

Contents

Foreword

The spiritual life—or asceticism, it is sometimes called—is an experience of the life of faith that the Church has been accumulating and transmitting from the beginning. This book contains what I have received from others, especially the founder of Opus Dei, St. Josemaría Escrivá. The rest comes from classical authors—Fathers of the Church, especially St. Gregory of Nyssa (d. ca. 386), Sts. Augustine and Cassian (d. 430 and 435), St. John Chrysostom (d. 407), and St. Gregory the Great (d. 604)—and writers such as St. Thomas Aquinas (d. 1274), St. Teresa of Avila, St. John of Avila, and St. John of the Cross (all sixteenth century), St. Francis de Sales (d. 1622), and many others. Among more recent authors I have made use of the writings of John Henry Newman, G. K. Chesterton, C. S. Lewis, Ronald Knox, Romano Guardini, and Josef Pieper; I also owe something to spiritual writers such as Eugene Boylan, Georges Chevrot, and Reginald Garrigou-Lagrange, among others. I have tried to cite sources in the simplest possible way to avoid overloading the text. Many of the citations from the founder of Opus Dei are simply given as the title of the book followed by the number of the point cited: *The Way*, *The Forge*, *Furrow*, *Christ Is Passing By*, *Friends of God*, *Conversations*, and *The Way of the Cross*.

This book is divided into two parts. The first deals with the manner of acquiring virtues. The second presents more directly some features of the life of Jesus that a Christian should conscientiously try to imitate.

The book does not propose an "ascetical method." It only tries to provide suggestions about the first steps in this path to the summit. One warning is necessary. I have mentioned the great gulf between wanting to do something and doing it. Ascetical theory is useless without ascetical practice. For the reading of this book to make sense, the reader must make resolutions and set objectives that will help him or her to advance, forever reviewing the objectives and renewing the journey.

Someone who lives like this will see that it is not complicated. The Christian life, like all life, has much spontaneity. Animals and plants grow by themselves, and the same happens here. No need to worry about all the details; the important thing is to keep moving ahead. And so the virtues will grow.

Anyone who begins this journey will find it a great experience that lends excitement to living. For God alone can be loved with enduring passion.

Introduction

Glory to God in the highest, and on earth peace among
men with whom he is pleased!

— Lk 2:14

St. Mark tells us in his Gospel (12:28) that, on one occasion,
a scribe approached our Lord and asked him: "What is the
greatest commandment?" Jesus answered him: "The first is
'Hear, O Israel: The Lord our God, the Lord is one; and you
shall love the Lord your God with all your heart, and with all
your soul, and with all your mind, and with all your strength.'"

These words would have been very familiar to Jesus' listeners for they were from the Law of Moses (Deut 6:4). The Jews
had the custom of reciting them as a prayer at least twice daily.
Yet the fact that the scribe asked this question—St. Matthew
tells us it was to test Jesus (Mt 23:35)—indicates that the
answer could have been different or that others would have
responded differently.

Today as then, this commandment is not easy to keep first
and foremost in daily life, where it must compete with many
interests. We may never have stopped to think of the enormous demands of these words: "You shall love the Lord your
God with your whole heart, with your whole soul, with your
whole mind, and with all your strength." But the principal and
most basic demand of the Christian life is to love God with
all our strength of soul and body.

This first commandment is inseparably united to a second: "You shall love your neighbor as yourself" (Mk 12:31; Lk 19:18). Our Lord later confirmed it with even greater force as a new commandment by telling his disciples to love one another as he himself loved them: that is, with the immense love of the heart of Christ who is God.

How can we love God with all our strength and our neighbor as ourselves, and, even more, with God's love? Are we capable of loving in this way? Is such an absolute love within our power?

The answer, based on the experience of many people who have made the effort throughout the centuries, is that such love is possible. But it is not a moment of ecstasy, nor is it enough simply to decide to do it. Rather, it is a matter of one's whole life. Only by a patient, constant, repeated, and thoughtful effort and with the help of God, can one become capable of loving God above all things and one's neighbor as oneself. It presupposes an extraordinary concentration of effort and involves all dimensions of human nature. Christian tradition calls that state sanctity: "He chose us in him before the foundation of the world, that we should be holy and blameless before him" (Eph 1:4). And it makes one similar to God himself: "He who loves is born of God and knows God. He who does not love does not know God; for God is love" (1 Jn 4:7–8); "God is love, and he who abides in love abides in God, and God abides in him" (1 Jn 4:16).

The sanctity that God expects of man is, in great part, God's pure gift—grace—which comes to us through Jesus Christ. "In this is love, not that we loved God but that he loved us and sent his Son to be the expiation for our sins" (1 Jn 4:10). But it also requires effort on the part of a human being, who tries little by little to overcome his limitations, to increase his capacities, to concentrate his strength, to love more and better each day.

From early times, Christian tradition has used an image based on the splendid theophany, a manifestation of God, which took place on Mount Sinai when God established with Moses a solemn covenant for the people of Israel. Ancient Christian writers such as Origen and St. Gregory of Nyssa saw in Moses's ascent to the mountain top an image of the purification the Christian has to accomplish to make himself capable of contemplating and loving God. St. John of the Cross uses the same image, although he calls the mountain Carmel in honor of the patrons of the Carmelite Order.

As in climbing a mountain, sanctification requires a systematic effort to reach the summit one step at a time. Thus the process of purification has been called asceticism, from the Greek word for effort or exercise. Yet one needn't imagine a very difficult climb or an exhausting effort. Neither Sinai nor Carmel is very steep, and both have fairly easy paths to the top. The important thing is to go up little by little, savoring the view, enjoying the scents of flowers, the width of the sky, the freshness of the breezes. It is also useful to have moments of rest and recuperation. The climb takes a little effort, but its beauties are compensation. And, in the case of Christian life, at the summit one contemplates not just a marvelous landscape but God himself.

God's grace is indispensable, but God gives this grace generously and, at the same time, mysteriously. It can bring the Christian to contemplation by new and unexpected paths, and it is given in a different way to each person. Trying to climb by oneself—leaving God aside—only leads to exhaustion, with an unbalanced personality at the end.

But what does it really mean in this context for someone to ascend? What makes a person better? Here we begin to enter into the marvelous world of the inner self—a universe even more exciting than the material universe whose beauties we scarcely know. Each person has within him or her an immense richness which is like a seed waiting to sprout. Only those who have been introduced to the world of the spirit know, by personal experience, that it exists. In a certain way, they themselves have brought it to life.

Such a person presents a very attractive image. Classic Greco-Roman education proposed as examples to new generations the most notable acts of valor, love of homeland, filial piety, and honesty of the greatest men. That wisdom of life was immensely enriched by Christian revelation, which provided, along with profound knowledge of the human being, a new model for humanity—Jesus Christ—and the power needed—the grace of God—to live by this model.

The key to interior growth is based on the fact that voluntary acts leave traces. We all know people who are very skillful at a variety of performances: craftsmen, athletes, musicians, etc. All have in common the ability to do easily and well what for others would be impossible or, at least, very difficult. They have mastered those techniques by repeating the same actions over and over again. The same rule applies in the education of the spirit: repetition. More than just training the body, this is formation of the spirit.

Both good and bad actions form customs and inclinations in the spirit, i.e., working habits. Good ones are called virtues, bad ones, vices. A good habit of the spirit is, for example, knowing how to decide without undue hurry and after considering the circumstances well. An opposed vice is rashness, which leads one to decide without thinking and to change one's decisions often and without a sound motive. "Will power" is precisely an assemblage of good habits attained after having repeated many acts oriented in the same direction.

Good habits, or virtues, lead to the dominance of the intellect in the life of the spirit. Vices disperse one's powers, whereas virtues concentrate them and place them at the service of the spirit. A person who has the vice of laziness can, perhaps, make wonderful resolutions, but is incapable of accomplishing them: his spirit has been harmed by laziness, by the resistance of his body. Students experience this conflict between what they propose to study and what they actually study. Merely to propose a thing does not mean one will be capable of carrying it out.

Only with effort—the frequent repetition of acts that cost us a little—does one acquire dominion over oneself. A virtuous person is capable, for example, of not eating something tasty that isn't good for him or her, or working when very tired or not getting upset over a trifle. Those without virtues, on the other hand, are more or less unable to act as they wish. They decide but fail to carry out what they decide.

Thus the person with virtues is much freer than the person without. The man without virtue may perhaps do "what he feels like," but "feeling like" is not freedom but slavery; whereas virtues extend the command of reason and the dominion of the will to the whole sphere of work. They concentrate a person's strength, enabling one to orient activity in the direction one desires. The very word virtue is related to the Latin words *vir* and *vis* meaning "man" and "strength." A man's real strength resides in his virtues. In contrast, small vices of conduct, such as the habit of not doing things when they should be done, weaken character and make a man incapable of living up to his ideals. They end by producing a mediocre personality.

Thus it should be clear why to love God above all things, to love him with all one's heart, with all one's soul, with all one's mind, with all one's strength, basically requires virtues. That is the aim of the ascetical or spiritual person: to form the virtues needed to bring all of one's strength to bear upon loving God and one's neighbor.

We have seen that the model of Christian asceticism is Jesus Christ. Although we cannot observe his daily behavior with our own eyes, we can learn a lot about him by reading the Gospels with attention. Christian life, however, not only takes Jesus Christ as a model but tends to identify with him, thinking what he thought, sharing his norms of conduct, acting as he would have done in our circumstances. In this regard the saints, those men and women who came closest to God, can also show us the face of our Lord. Yet that identification is partly unconscious, since the action of God in us, his grace, spontaneously produces that effect. St. Paul expresses this mystery in many ways, but especially when, having reached human and Christian maturity, he exclaims: "I have been crucified with Christ; it is no longer I who live, but Christ who lives in me" (Gal 2:20). And, again, when he tells the Ephesians of his hopes for them: "that Christ may dwell in your hearts through faith; that you, being rooted and grounded in love, may have power to comprehend with all the saints what is the breadth and length and height and depth, and to know the love of Christ which surpasses knowledge, that you may be filled with all the fullness of God" (Eph 3:17–19). This identification with Christ is the goal of Christian asceticism.

Part One

VIRTUES

And if anyone loves righteousness, her labors are virtues; for she teaches self-control and prudence, justice and courage; nothing in life is more profitable for men than these.

— Wis 8:7

In this first part of the book, divided into thirteen chapters, we look at the fundamental aspects of the interior life.

The first three touch on general points of character. The sense of the presence of God (chapt. 1) leads us to see God in everything, to know that he is close and to keep him there, as the end of our actions. Self-knowledge (chapt. 2) gives us information about the state in which we find ourselves, and the steps we have to take to improve. Knowing our deficiencies leads us to the ascetical struggle (chapt. 3). In that chapter we deal with the importance of improving each day a little and returning to begin again whenever necessary. Then we go on to describe the virtues. First are those which free us from the strongest passions: laziness, love of comfort, sensuality, and pride. These virtues—fortitude, detachment, chastity, and humility—are those we must acquire first, to attain interior freedom and the ability to love God.

The two following chapters refer to virtues that convey a special outlook: simplicity and cheerfulness. These tend to show themselves as soon as the ascetical life starts to grow. Later we speak of two central virtues: prudence, the virtue proper to the intellect which refers to the capacity to choose well, and integrity, which is the virtue proper to the will and refers to a love for one's duties. Both of these, but especially the second, indicate the crowning of spiritual growth. The chapter called "Living for Others" deals with a basic orientation that the life of a Christian should have; while chapter 13, "Work," deals with the activity to which we dedicate the greater part of life, the basic service we provide to others, and a place were we have to meet God in this world.

1.

The Sense of the Presence of God

One of the most beautiful incidents in the Acts of the Apostles is St. Paul's address to the Athenians. After preaching for several days around the town, he was invited to explain his teachings in the Areopagus, where citizens of that cultured city liked to gather to converse. There, using the resources of classical rhetoric, which he knew well, Paul began a marvelous discourse, speaking first of what God is and then going on to speak of the Redemption through Jesus Christ. His address was not successful. The Athenians mocked him when they heard him speak of the resurrection of the dead. He only obtained a few conversions (Acts 17:16–34).

The skeptical Athenians could not accept the idea that Christ had been able to rise from the dead. But regarding even the first part of the address, there were great differences despite apparent agreement. This is how Paul speaks about God: "The God who made the world and everything in it, being Lord of heaven and earth . . . gives to all men life and breath. . . . And he made from one every nation of men to live on all the face of the earth . . . that they should seek God, in the hope that they might feel after him and find him. Yet he is not far from each of us."

In this admirable summary, Paul presents three essential elements of Christian theology about God. God created all things and is, therefore, Lord of all; God created man for himself, so that he could know and love him; to encounter God is possible because "he is not far from each of us."

One finds this same idea many centuries earlier in another beautiful discourse, in which Moses reminds the people of the great care that God had shown for them. "What great nation is there that has a god so near to it as the Lord our God is to us, whenever we call upon him?" (Deut 4:7).

God is much nearer for us than for those Greek listeners of St. Paul, whose ideas about God were rather confused. We Christians know that the world exists because God wishes it, not only wished it at the first moment, but wishes it now. The world depends at every moment on the divine will. Therefore God is behind everything that exists. Fundamental to the existence of each thing is the activity of God, who wants that thing to be.

This is the theological foundation of the presence of God. God is behind the activity of things and therefore behind historical events. Nothing happens that was not foreseen or willed by God. The world is not governed by blind fate but by the design of an intelligent being, infinitely powerful and good. Christian tradition calls this plan of God "Divine Providence."

These two convictions, that God is present in all things (divine omnipresence) and that God is behind all events (divine providence), give Christians a special, new way of being in the world.

The world is not dominated by dark, evil forces, as the most important ancient civilizations thought. It is something good that has come from the hands of a good God and shows his greatness. "The heavens are telling the glory of God; and the firmament proclaims his handiwork" (Ps 19:1). In this world, man can meet God, because "ever since the creation of the world his invisible nature, namely, his eternal power and deity, has been clearly perceived in the things that have been made" (Rom 1:20).

These convictions of faith should be pervasive in the conduct of the Christian. If our aim is to get to know God with our whole heart, with our whole soul, with all our strength, we should become accustomed to seeing him behind whatever is and happens. "Behold, I stand at the door and knock; if any one hears my voice and opens the door, I will come in to him and eat with him, and he with me" (Rev 3:20).

It is not necessary to seek special times or places. It is enough to want to speak with him. "The Lord is near to all who call upon him, to all who call upon him in truth" (Ps 144:18). But it requires a certain maturity to have this sense of the presence of God.

The Judaeo-Christian tradition has understood the sense of the presence of God in two ways: first, seeing God behind his creatures; second, knowing oneself to be a creature of God and therefore in God's presence. Psalm 139 expresses this in an eminent way: "O Lord, thou hast searched me and known me! Thou knowest when I sit down and when I rise up; thou discernest my thoughts from afar. Thou searchest out my path and my lying down, and art acquainted with all my ways. Even before a word is on my tongue, lo, O Lord, thou knowest it altogether. . . . Whither shall I go from thy Spirit? Or whither shall I flee from thy presence? If I ascend to heaven, thou art there! If I make my bed in Sheol, thou art there! If I take the wings of the morning and dwell in the uttermost parts of the sea, even there thy hand shall lead me, and thy right hand shall hold me" (Ps 139:1–10).

Christian iconography sometimes expresses this by representing God as an all-seeing eye. But that look is not accusing: it is the look of a Father affectionately observing what his children are doing. If we accustom ourselves to the idea that God is at our side, we will find it easy to speak with him during the day and our activity will be saturated with his presence.

Another consideration also can help: God is in things and in events. St. John of the Cross says creatures are "like a trace of the footsteps of God" (*Spiritual Canticle*, 5:3). It is easy to see God in the marvels of nature, the vast panoramas, the harmonies of color of the sky and the earth, the serenity of the forests, the clamor of storms, the immensity of the oceans. But we must see him also in the most ordinary realities, the ordinary circumstances of life. As if wishing to balance the lyricism of her fellow Carmelite, St. John, St. Teresa reminds us that "the Lord also walks among the pots and pans" (*Foundations*, 5:8). It is up to us to find him there. "He is not far," St. Augustine says, "Love and he will come near you, love and he will live in you" (*Sermon*, 21).

This sense of the presence of God is the first step in asceticism. A close relationship with him allows us to advance step by step on the path that leads to loving him with all our strength. But it is not enough merely to say, "I want to live in the presence of God." We must create a habit by repeated acts, returning many times to fundamental convictions: God sees me; God is behind all things and events.

The practical problem of keeping these things in mind was considered by the early Christians, meditating on our Lord's saying, "that they ought always to pray and not lose heart" (Lk 18:1). How is it possible continually to recall God when we are so easily distracted? The solution they found—still valid today—was the frequent recitation of short prayers—petitions, exclamations, and acts of prayer that they called ejaculations or aspirations.

St. Augustine tells us that in his day this was already an old tradition among the Egyptian hermits. Later, it extended throughout all of Eastern Christianity, and later throughout the West. The Eastern monks have a strong affection for this practice, which they have developed and made a basic point of their spirituality. So, for example, from them come the custom of repeating "Christ have mercy on us, Lord have mercy on us, Christ have mercy on us," the passage from the liturgy of Good Friday (*Hagios o Theos*) translated in the West as "Holy God, Holy Strong One, Holy Immortal One, free us O Lord from all evil," and the now traditional "Glory be to the Father, and to the Son, and to the Holy Spirit."

Useful as it is to repeat very simple prayers, we don't have to repeat prayers of others. We can use thoughts such as: Lord, help me! Lord, give me more faith! Lord, increase my charity! Lord, make me faithful to you! We must deal with God like children. "In praying do not heap up empty phrases as the Gentiles do; for they think that they will be heard for their many words. Do not be like them, for your Father knows what you need before you ask him" (Mt 6:7–8).

At times, aspirations can be joined to small actions including very ordinary ones. In some places it was said that an egg should be boiled for the time it took to say two Our Fathers. In this way the faith penetrated the details of life. We can do something similar, making entering or leaving our home, beginning or ending work, or eating meals occasions for aspirations. Getting up in the morning and going to bed at night are suitable moments. Any task that is somewhat mechanical or repetitive can be an occasion for praying aspirations.

The effort to attain a sense of the presence of God produces an interesting psychological effect: one's interior monologue is transformed into a dialogue with God. The effect is splendid. For, while the monologue tends to deform reality by exaggerating aspects favorable to us and obscuring those which show our weaknesses, the dialogue with God makes our spirit crystal-clear and transparent, so that the best that is in us emerges naturally in our conduct and expression. Life becomes filled with the brightness of the divine.

The effort to remember God produces marvelous fruit. Here is how the founder of Opus Dei expressed it: "First one brief aspiration, then another, and another . . . till our fervor seems insufficient, because words are too poor. . . . Then this gives way to intimacy with God, looking at God without needing rest or feeling tired. We begin to live as captives, as prisoners. And while we carry out as perfectly as we can (with all our mistakes and limitations) the tasks allotted to us by our situation and duties, our soul longs to escape. It is drawn towards God like iron drawn by a magnet. One begins to love Jesus, in a more effective way, with the sweet and gentle surprise of his encounter" (*Friends of God*, no. 296).

2.

Self-Knowledge

On the giant door of the Temple of Apollo in Delphos, one of the wonders of the ancient world, was an inscription that was something of a summary of classic wisdom: "Know Thyself." Surprising as it might seem today, the maxim did not refer so much to discovering one's own marvelous qualities as to becoming aware of one's serious limitations.

It's said that the best business in the world would be buying men at what they're worth and selling them at what they think they're worth. When others don't have the good sense to accept our superiority, there follow hurt feelings, rancor, sadness, anger, vengeance, insolence, disputes . . . the things that break down peace in families, communities, and nations.

On the other hand, self-knowledge is the best path for understanding others. The best place for each of us to study human feelings is our own interior experience. One who has experienced suffering understands what it is to suffer; one who suffers a setback knows what it is to be sad; one who feels abandoned understands loneliness. And so on for the gamut of feelings that can occupy the human heart. In knowing oneself better, one becomes better able to understand others because one "knows" what is happening to them.

Even so, the most important thing about self-knowledge is that it is indispensable for dealing with God. Before God, we are all very small; and only one who knows himself to be small is in a position to converse with him. It is a constant in the lives of saints that they felt more unworthy of God as they drew nearer to him. Their growing love of God helped them see more clearly their infidelity to him.

Recognition of one's limitations appears to be a prerequisite of getting closer to God. Pascal made this one of his pivotal ideas. The sense of sin, of one's own unworthiness, and the sense of God go hand in hand. Where the sense of sin has vanished, the sense of God disappears: there is, in the words of Martin Buber, "an eclipse of God."

"Knowledge of oneself," says St. John of the Cross, "is the first step that has to be taken for the soul to reach the knowledge of God" (*Spiritual Canticle*, 4, 1). Nothing separates one from God more than the inability to recognize one's limitations in his sight. This is the meaning of one of Jesus' most beautiful parables. "Two men went up into the temple to pray, one a Pharisee and the other a tax collector. The Pharisee stood and prayed thus with himself, 'God, I thank thee that I am not like other men, extortioners, unjust, adulterers, or even like this tax collector. I fast twice a week, I give tithes of all that I get.' But the tax collector, standing far off, would not even lift up his eyes to heaven, but beat his breast, saying, 'God, be merciful to me a sinner!' I tell you, this man went down to his house justified rather than the other" (Lk 18:9–14).

The Pharisee really did fast twice a week and pay his tithes scrupulously. But he went up to the temple to sing his own praises. And he returned home without meeting God, because he hadn't really sought him. The publican was really a sinner, but he repented and thus encountered God. A man who is honest about himself is prepared to be honest with God.

It is not wrong to acknowledge our good points, though without the vanity of the Pharisee. Knowing the talents God has given us should lead us to thank him and to make good use of them. "Everyone to whom much is given, of him will much be required" (Lk 12:48). Knowledge of the gifts of God should be a spur to serve God better and a source of new reasons for repentance. This is what happens in the lives of saints. Self-knowledge is indispensable in the journey of the interior life by which we aim to reach the summit of love of God.

Here is the meaning of a very old, very necessary practice of the ascetical life: the examination of conscience. This consists in a daily checking—because life flees from our grasp on a daily basis—of how we have behaved toward God. It is an occasion to thank him for his gifts and ask pardon for our sins and lack of correspondence.

This can be done in a thousand ways; and there are also special methods (those of St. Ignatius, St. Francis de Sales, and the Sulpician method). But it is not something complex. It is very simple. First consider for a moment that one is in the presence of God and wishes to make this examination with the light he himself gives. Ask his help. Then mentally review the day. This can be done hour by hour or under subject headings. There are many different possibilities: how did my work go, my prayer, my dealings with others; what did I do in thought, word, and deed; how did I carry out my duties toward God, neighbor, self, etc.?

The founder of Opus Dei sometimes recommended a very simple examination: What did I do well—then give thanks to God for that; what did I do badly—then ask forgiveness for what I failed in; what could I have done better—then make a resolution to improve next day.

The method is not so important, though it can help. What's important is the desire to get to specifics and ask forgiveness. It is not enough to see oneself as a kind of generic "sinner." *How* do I sin? *How* do I fail in love of God? There is no correcting faults one does not recognize. We need to discover each day the details of our laziness, the specific lacks of attention to others, the big or small compromises with sensuality, excesses in speaking, in eating, etc. We have to get to the reasons for that bad humor, that sharp response, that negligence, that apathy which holds us back. Probably there will be no surprising discoveries, and we will conclude that our faults were due to pride, laziness, or sensuality. But it is important to be specific and feel ashamed.

Having placed ourselves in the presence of God and examined our day, we come to the most important moment of the examination: contrition, sorrow for having abused God's love. "Have mercy on me, O God, according to thy steadfast love; according to thy abundant mercy blot out my transgressions. Wash me thoroughly from my iniquity, and cleanse me from my sin! For I know my transgressions, and my sin is ever before me. Against thee, thee only, have I sinned, and done that which is evil in thy sight" (Ps 51:1–4). Repentance comes at once if we have done the examination well in the presence of God. And its finest fruit is a resolution to avoid repeating that sin.

An examination of conscience done well helps one go forward with security, while an examination of conscience badly done has bad consequences. Love is strong because it urges one toward heroism, but it is very sensitive because it can cool off quickly through negligence and lack of care. The love of God is especially demanding. Says St. Augustine, "As soon as you are satisfied with yourself, there you will stop. If you say, 'that's enough,' you are lost" (*Sermon*, 169). Examination of conscience carried out well will give us each day a greater impetus to love God passionately and efficaciously.

3.

The Ascetical Struggle

The Spanish physician and literary figure Gregorio Marañon wrote in his *Ensayos Liberales* that "the most human disposition of youthful virtue is a generous rejection of all that is imperfect—which is practically the whole of life—in other words, rebellion" (Madrid 1966, 90).

The mind of youth is a moment for great ambitions and adventures. Yet, even in youth not everything is positive. Young people lack the experience necessary to channel enthusiasm and self-giving. Often, too, they lack the strength of will needed to sustain the effort to follow up and follow through.

In contrast, a mature person knows his or her limitations; he has learned to measure his strength and use it well. His projects are no longer so ambitious, but he is able to accomplish them. Nevertheless, with the passage from youth to maturity a change sets in: one begins to lose that "generous rejection of the imperfect" and grow resigned. One is satisfied with much less: a little money, a little time, a little tranquility, a few comforts.

This fading away of ideals takes place in the lives of many men and women (although some never had any ideals). It is one of the clearest signs of the chasm that so often separates desires from capacities. A young woman wants to eliminate hunger from the world, but she has to concentrate on her studies. A young man is distressed by the problem of homelessness, but he can't resist buying himself a high-powered motorcycle and spending a month of his vacation at the beach just working on his tan. The history of the generation of '68 is a graphic example of the fading away of ideals that were never put into effect.

Great ideals are not enough. The ability to work well is essential. The first thing that has to change for this world to improve is ourselves. Not that we must be perfect before doing anything, for if that were the case we would never begin. But unless serious about remedying our own defects, we will do very little to solve those of the world. We will sow our mediocrity through our works.

The examination of conscience of which we spoke in the previous chapter gives us an idea of our many mistakes and our resistance to improving. St. Paul expressed it very well: "For I do not do the good I want, but the evil I do not want is what I do. So I find it to be a law that when I want to do right, evil lies close at hand. For I delight in the law of God, in my inmost self, but I see in my members another law at war with the law of my mind and making me captive to the law of sin" (Rom 7:19–23).

There is another me inside each of us: we are not as we want to be, we often act as we have resolved not to act. These are the traces of our sins, which have their origin in the mysterious wounds of original sin.

Those disordered tendencies inclining us to laziness, sensuality, and pride, have traditionally been called passions. Examination of conscience done well helps us see these things as they are present in our life. That is the first step toward improving.

Passions are tendencies that tend to deceive us. They suggest that it is too difficult to do things (laziness); they invest corporal goods (comfort, food, sex, etc.) with exaggerated charm; they make us believe we are worth much more than we really are (pride). If we let them lead us, our behavior becomes deformed. That is vice. Virtue lies in doing what we understand we ought to do, even though we don't feel like it, and not doing what we should not do, even though we do feel like it; and to know how to stay in my place and recognize my limitations. It is in the effort to organize one's life this way that the ascetical struggle principally consists.

This is a struggle that never ends. It is important to enter it with a sporting spirit. St. Augustine expressed it in a very lively way: "Then we have to struggle always, because this inclination toward sin with which we have been born cannot end as long as we live: it can decrease, but not be extinguished, and the saints take part in this struggle for their whole lives" (*Sermon*, 151). Victory is by no means instantaneous, and some days are not so good as others. But the daily struggle makes life interesting. Even when defeated, we begin again, like good athletes. What matters is not giving up.

We need a certain strategy in this battle, because we can't make gains on all fronts at once. Here we have a traditional resource called the particular examination. This involves choosing from among the points where we see ourselves most often weakening, the one that seems most important. One makes a very specific resolution for improvement on that point and considers it daily. For example, someone who sees that his weak point is laziness might fix his particular examination on being punctual and setting to work at two or three particular times each day. If someone else talks too much and interrupts other people, the resolution might be to listen more to what others say instead of speaking oneself. The important thing is that it be something concrete, and to examine oneself on this point each day.

We can designate our own particular examination and change it after a few days (or weeks), when we see we are improving (or perhaps that we aren't). Nevertheless, it is a big help if some other person—a spiritual director, someone with experience in the ascetical life—counsels us. If one usually goes to Confession to the same priest, he might be able to give advice. The interior struggle requires much motivation, for there will be times of fatigue, real or apparent defeat, and perplexity. The counsel and support of another person who knows us well, loves us, and knows something of what it is to love God helps a lot. St. John of the Cross likens the soul attempting to go it alone to "an ignited coal which is alone: it is more likely to go out than to keep burning."

And if one stops fighting? Then the result is a crisis of indifference. This weariness of spirit leads one to seek alternatives that give greater satisfactions than the struggle to which love of God is directed. That state is called tepidity, a sickness of the spirit. But an examination, well carried out, with a true discovery of our errors and authentic sorrow for them, can refresh love of God and restore the sporting tone of the ascetical struggle whose characteristic fruit is, paradoxically, peace of soul.

4.

Fortitude

One way the "old man" whom we carry within us shows himself is by our complaints in the face of anything that requires effort. They usually are accompanied by false excuses: "It's getting late," "You've already worked too long," "Tomorrow will be better for doing this," "The others aren't doing as much." By giving in, we create habits and become more and more useless, incapable of any serious work of body or spirit.

This defect—which we all have in seed form—is laziness: a horror of anything that demands effort. It is remarkably effective. Apparently trivial, it's the root of many great problems. Many evils in the world are basically caused by negligence: reluctance to undertake what is difficult, apathy in the fulfillment of obligations in the service of others, refusal to make the sacrifice it would take to apply a remedy to a bad situation.

To do what is good requires courage, that is, the ability to make demands on oneself and overcome the fear of suffering, of work, of effort. Everything of value comes at a cost. If we want to do something, we must overcome the resistance of our own body to moving itself, the resistance of things to being moved, and very often, the resistance of people our movement bothers and displeases. Our Lord knew this. "Enter by the narrow gate; for the gate is wide and the way is easy, that leads to destruction, and those who enter by it are many. For the gate is narrow and the way is hard, that leads to life" (Mt 7:13–14).

Weak men are sometimes mistaken for good ones. True, someone trying to live a Christian life is affable, forgiving, and generally has peaceful behavior. But in a man of God, that temperament tends to be united to fortitude, for serving God is often costly. Take St. Paul: "Five times I have received at the hands of the Jews the forty lashes less one. Three times I have been beaten with rods; once I was stoned. Three times I have been shipwrecked; a night and a day I have been adrift at sea; on frequent journeys, in danger from rivers, danger from robbers, danger from my own people, danger from Gentiles, danger in the city, danger in the wilderness, danger at sea, danger from false brethren; in toil and hardship, through many a sleepless night, in hunger and thirst, often without food, in cold and exposure. And, apart from other things, there is the daily pressure upon me of my anxiety for all the churches" (2 Cor 11:24–28). God doesn't ask this much of everyone. But without a little of that courage, we couldn't take a step in his service: "Be strong, and let your heart take courage, all you who wait for the Lord!" (Ps 30:24).

It has been said that wars are won by tired soldiers. The capacity to make demands on oneself is the key to success in many activities: sports, music, dance, business, study—all require a lot of sacrifice. The same is true of Christian life: "Tender, soft, flabby . . . : that's not the way I want you. It's about time you got rid of that peculiar pity you feel for yourself" (*The Way*, no. 193).

It is necessary to expect difficulties and not attach too much importance to the body's resistance. "Do not think of complaining about the weaknesses and minor ailments from

which women suffer," says St. Teresa to her nuns, "for the
devil sometimes makes you imagine them. They come and go;
and unless you get rid of the habit of talking about them and
complaining of everything (except to God), you will never
come to the end of them. . . . For this body of ours has one
fault: the more you indulge it, the more things it discovers to
be essential to it" (*The Way of Perfection*, 11, 3).

Yes, it is necessary to take care of the body. It would be
foolish to jeopardize one's health needlessly. But it isn't good
to go to the opposite extreme, using the slightest infirmity—a
cold, a slight fever, a minor discomfort—as an excuse for
shirking our duties.

St. Teresa tells of her own experience: "As my own health
is so bad, I was always impeded by my fears, and my devotion
was of no value at all until I resolved not to worry any more
about my body or my health; and now I trouble about them
very little. For it pleased God to reveal to me this device of
the devil; and so, whenever the devil suggested that I should
ruin my health, I would reply: 'Even if I die it is of little consequence.' 'Rest, indeed!' I would say. 'I need no rest; what I
need is crosses.' And so with other things. I saw clearly that
in very many cases, although in fact I have very bad health, it
was a temptation either of the devil or of my own weakness;
and since I have been less self-regarding and indulgent my
health has been very much better" (*Life*, 13:7). Prudence, seeing things in the presence of God, will guide how we should
act in each case with respect to health.

We must learn to be unyielding with ourselves in whatever concerns the fulfillment of our duties: work, study, our
family duties, etc. That includes acknowledging the deception
that leads us to postpone what costs us, to begin with what
we like most, to stop doing things when they become boring,
or systematically to leave things for tomorrow. "Tomorrow!
Sometimes it is prudence; very often it is the adverb of the

defeated" (*The Way*, no. 251). We have to overcome indulgence, negligence, and idleness, and get on with our obligations.

People often tell themselves, "Others don't do as much as I do." But instead of comparing down, we ought to compare up, measuring ourselves by those who do more than we do—sometimes with ignoble motives. We who are moved by love of God shouldn't lack the energy to make demands on ourselves.

This is one of the keys to the ascetical life. To make demands on oneself, not in a fanatical way but simply to carry out what one honorably sees one ought to do, involves overcoming those treacherous resistances inspired by the lower part of one's nature. It means learning not to fool oneself, cutting out interior excuses by the roots, unmasking the artificial reasons that centering on comfort raises: in short, imposing the order of the intellect over the resistance offered by the body.

A person who makes demands on himself also is entitled to make demands on others when necessary. And it *is* necessary in almost all tasks of direction, government, and education. Often it is a duty. Otherwise, the toleration of unjust behavior harms the business enterprise or public institution or family. Spoiling children by always giving them just what they want is an instance. This produces an individual who demands a lot of others but has very little capacity to make demands on himself. Life may straighten him out in time, but it would have saved everyone a lot of unpleasantness if his parents had done the job at the start.

Fortitude is one of the most attractive attributes of the human personality. The ancients, desiring that their glory be celebrated by posterity, were moved by fortitude to practice heroism. The Christian, on the other hand, should cultivate fortitude out of love for God, which has always been one of the motives of heroism. When we feel discouragement in the face of difficulties we need to raise our eyes and recall with

St. Paul that, "I can do all things in him who strengthens me," adding in the words of the psalmist, "thou art my rock and my fortress" (Ps 31:4). Says St. Teresa of Avila: "His Majesty desires and loves courageous souls, if they have no confidence in themselves but walk in humility; and I have never seen any such person hanging back on this road" (*Life*, 13, 2).

5.

Detachment

Some scenes in the Gospel leave you feeling as you do when something expected to turn out well ends badly instead. That's how it is with the rich young man. St. Mark reports that a young man approached our Lord and, kneeling, asked what he should do to gain eternal life. Jesus told him to keep the commandments. "Teacher, all these I have observed from my youth," he replied. Looking upon him and loving him, Jesus then said: "You lack one thing; go, sell what you have, and give to the poor, and you will have treasure in heaven; and come, follow me" (Mk 10:17–22). And then the disappointment: "At that saying his countenance fell, and he went away sorrowful; for he had great possessions."

"How hard it will be for those who trust in riches to enter the kingdom of God!" Jesus reflects (Mk 10:23). St. Mark says the disciples were "amazed at his words." But our Lord wished to give them a lesson: the young man was undoubtedly good, but love of his possessions still carried more weight than his love of God.

The goods of this earth—money, social position, prestige— have great power to attract our hearts, which were made for God. But our Lord leaves no doubt. "No one can serve two masters. . . . You cannot serve God and mammon" (Mt 6:24). And "whoever of you does not renounce all that he has cannot be my disciple" (Lk 14:33).

If we are careless, money can control our lives, even if we don't intend it. Many people now take it for granted that the purpose of life is to have more and live better. This ambition tends to grow and can end up occupying first place in one's life, even though one may not face up to that fact. People devote themselves to the quest for material goods: success in business, a second home, travel, investments. And at the end there has been no time for seeking things theoretically acknowledged as more important: family life, friendship, culture . . . and above all a relationship with God. Think of the parable of the sower: "And as for what fell among the thorns, they are those who hear, but as they go on their way they are choked by the cares and riches and pleasures of life, and their fruit does not mature" (Lk 8:14).

It is a trap to think that "later" (after getting this or that) one will begin to live differently. "The land of a rich man brought forth plentifully; and he thought to himself, 'What shall I do, for I have nowhere to store my crops?' And he said, 'I will do this: I will pull down my barns, and build larger ones; and there I will store all my grain and my goods. And I will say to my soul, 'Soul, you have ample goods laid up for many years; take your ease, eat, drink, be merry.' But God said to him, 'Fool! This night your soul is required of you; and the things you have prepared, whose will they be?' So is he who lays up treasure for himself, and is not rich toward God" (Lk 12:16–21).

This world will end, and it is essential to keep that in mind. This is one of the reasons why there arose in the Church a special way of living poverty, the consecrated life. By their renunciation of the possession of goods, their vow of poverty for love of God, those in consecrated life give witness that our world is passing away, and we must live with our thoughts on eternity.

God does not ask everyone to live poverty the same way, but he does ask that we not allow our hearts to focus on the goods of the earth so that we end up adoring them like idols. The end of human life is not material well-being but the love of God. We are in this world to seek him and serve others. The world is something good, which came from the hands of God and which God has handed over to us to care for it and use its goods as needed. And we plainly do need food, clothing, shelter, health care, culture, and much else.

Material goods, then, are instruments that help us to attain the ends of our life: to encounter God and to serve others. Yet the attractiveness of money or of power is so great that it tends to disguise itself as something noble. How many parents need to be reminded that it is more important to give time to their children than to work more to provide them with superfluous comforts!

To the extent work brings surplus goods, there is a greater moral obligation to use them in service of others. At all times, says St. Augustine, the approach to things should be marked by "the temperance of one who uses them not . . . the eagerness of one who puts his heart into them" (*De moribus Eccl. Cath.*, 1, 21, 39). So, for instance, a house is a home where family life takes place (an "instrument" for family life), one's car is an "instrument" of work and relaxation, and so on. This way of seeing things is a safeguard against the spirit of luxury, the love of goods for themselves, which often brings with it envy of those who have more and ostentation in showing off one's own goods. A person who wants to serve God and others must aim to have sober tastes. He should live with what is necessary, avoid whims, and have an austere temperament. This is to say he must practice detachment.

To see things as instruments does not mean mistreating them. On the contrary, the redemption worked by Christ, realized in the world through us, demands that our surroundings be attractive, congenial, cheerful, and inviting. This is an external sign that God is near, that the truth can be found here; and the truth is always accompanied by good taste. Christian poverty and detachment have nothing to do with dirtiness, carelessness, or disorder. Except in some extreme cases, these are signs of laziness.

Seeing things as instruments leads one to think carefully before buying something (so as not to be burdened down with useless things) and to care for things so that they last. What is simple, useful, and attractive is preferred.

As for surplus goods, inherited or earned, these are new responsibilities, to be used well in the service of others, first of all those who have least. "If any one has the world's goods and sees his brother in need, yet closes his heart against him, how does God's love abide in him?" (1 Jn 3:17). No one can solve all the problems in the world, but helping the people around us may be possible.

At the same time, someone with great wealth can undertake or collaborate in great enterprises of service. A Catholic also should be aware of the Church's many programs of social assistance, education, etc., and should support them generously.

Austerity and simplicity should mark all aspects of our lives—for example, the use of free time, watching television and other recreations, our physical comforts. Everything should be measured by the standard of reason.

Under this heading, we should give attention to our eating and drinking. Virtue does not consist in depriving ourselves of food and drink, but in eating and drinking as a human being should. "You generally eat more than you need. And that fullness, which often causes you physical heaviness and discomfort, benumbs your mind and renders you unfit to taste supernatural treasures. What a fine virtue, even for this earth, temperance is!" (*The Way*, no. 682). It is a good rule of thumb to eat a little less than you would like to eat. Passions deceive.

If we always eat until we are filled, we will end up harming ourselves and wasting time.

Compromises in this area, though perhaps unimportant in themselves, can lead to others that are important. St. Thomas Aquinas skillfully enumerates the excesses (*S.Th.*, I–II, q. 77, a.9, ad 2): avidity, gluttony, too much time spent preparing meals, the search for exquisiteness in dishes, eating at inopportune times. "Gluttony is an ugly vice. Don't you feel a bit amused and even disgusted, when you see a group of dignified gentlemen, seated solemnly around a table, stuffing fatty substances into their stomachs, with an air of ritual, as if that were an end in itself?" (*The Way*, no. 679).

As for alcoholic drink, it is hardly a secret how dangerous excess can be. Be prepared; avoid repeating others' mistakes; know yourself; set and keep limits; stick to a little less that the moderate drinkers drink.

The moral gravity of gluttony and excessive drinking can be difficult to measure in a specific instance, but it can be seen very clearly when the excess takes control of somebody's life. "For many, of whom I have often told you and now tell you even with tears, live as enemies of the cross of Christ. Their end is destruction, their god is the belly, and they glory in their shame, with minds set on earthly things" (Phil 3:18–19).

Living with moderation enables us to live as free men, with a strong spirit and even good health. Detachment and sobriety give life a tone that is unmistakably Christian and are the basis for cultivating the most important virtues that lead to love of God. Says St. Paul: "I have learned, in whatever state I am, to be content. I know how to be abased, and I know how to abound; in any and all circumstances I have learned the secret of facing plenty and hunger, abundance and want. I can do all things in him who strengthens me" (Phil 4:11–13).

6.

Chastity

"God created man in his own image, in the image of God he created him; male and female he created them. And God blessed them, and God said to them, 'Be fruitful and multiply, and fill the earth and subdue it'" (Gen 1:27–28). With these solemn words, the sacred writer communicates the Christian understanding of the human person—his dignity, his sexual differentiation, and finally the blessing of God, which gives meaning to that sexual differentiation ordained to the transmission of life.

Marriage from its origin is a union between a man and a woman, open by its very nature to fruitfulness. The sexual differentiation between man and woman has that end and the sexual faculties are ordained to accomplish it. This is part of human nature. Man and woman feel a mutual inclination to a conjugal relationship from which new lives have their origin. This is a matter of a natural mechanism partly outside of our control and also partly under our control.

The sexual instinct is the strongest instinct next to that of survival. But for human beings, unlike animals, it is subject to a certain extent to the rule of the spirit. Man is called to control his sexual activity by the use of reason.

This is not so easy. As a consequence of original sin, human appetites are disordered. This may be even more true of the sexual instinct than of the others (the desire to eat, the desire for comfort, etc.). The intellect governs this instinct—and, in general, all of the passions—in an indirect way. Aristotle says it exercises only a political power over the passions and not a despotic power, he uses as an example a charioteer driving a team of horses. The horses obey him, but only to a certain extent, maintaining a desire for autonomy.

So, for example, a man may decide to start seeing a woman and fall in love. Falling in love is to a certain extent a natural reaction: a man cannot fall in love simply by an act of the will. But he can choose to place himself into the occasion of falling in love. If, later, he comes to think the woman is not suitable for him, he may decide to distance himself from her (in spite of feeling that he loves her), and in this way forget her little by little; or he may fall in love with someone else. The example illustrates a mix of natural reactions (impossible to control directly) with governance by the intellect. The instinctive response to certain stimuli cannot be directly controlled; but it can be indirectly controlled by controlling the stimuli. This is how the intellect establishes order in regard to sexual desire. And this habitual order is chastity: the capacity to control the desire for sexual pleasure.

Marriage, however, is much more than a sexual relationship. It is a relationship between two intelligent human beings united by a special friendship. And here is where new lives ordinarily originate and find the human and material resources necessary to grow to maturity. Thus, the family—married couple plus children—is an institution of vital importance for society. Sexuality, therefore, affects man very deeply and is the nucleus of social life. This is why sexual discipline has always been an imperative for any healthy society, including non-Christian ones, whereas lack of that discipline is a symptom of social collapse.

Christian teaching on this point is extremely clear. Sexual life is constitutive of marriage, and sexual pleasure is only licit there and must be open to the generation of new lives. Our society trivializes sex to the point of treating it as one more item of consumption. But this trivializing leads directly to the trivialization of love. And to trivialize love (the most noble of personal human relationships) makes it impossible to enjoy the happiness that it can produce (love between spouses, love in family life, friendship).

In that case all that is left is the satisfaction of instinct. Today an enormous industry—including many aspects of literary and artistic production—lives by exploiting a certain physical pleasure. (Suppose similar pleasure came from blowing one's nose: would there be a whole industry devoted to exploiting *that*?)

But let's not fool ourselves. None of us is beyond being tempted. We need to take seriously the words of Holy Scripture: "Do not be deceived; neither the immoral . . . nor adulterers, nor homosexuals . . . will inherit the kingdom of God" (1 Cor 6:9–10). The fact is that essential dimensions of life are in play here.

Human happiness and the kingdom of heaven are such serious matters that it is worth the effort to live well. In the face of assaults on our intimate selves delivered through the media and advertising, we have to react—not least, because we know there is something in us disposed to give in. Experience should teach us how to improve.

The central issue is love. Where there is true love, one will find the strength necessary to live sexuality in an ordered way. In a precious document on priestly celibacy, Paul VI said: "Love, when it is genuine, is all-embracing, stable and lasting, an irresistible spur to all forms of heroism." When love is great, pure, and generous, it has the strength to combat the lower desires, which are always mean and egoistic.

Through love of God one can reach the point of giving up all the satisfactions of married life and the exercise of sexuality. St. Paul says: "I wish that all were as I myself am. But each has his own special gift from God, one of one kind and one of another. To the unmarried and the widows I say that it is well for them to remain single as I do" (1 Cor 7:7–8). In this way, he explained, they could dedicate themselves more easily to the things of God (1 Cor 7:32–35). In the Church from the beginning there have been people who decided to live celibate lives, thus imitating Jesus and dedicating their energies to the service of the Church. Soon it became the custom to choose from among these men bishops, and later priests, until that custom spread throughout the whole Latin Church. Today, in addition to many reasons of dedication and efficiency, apostolic celibacy (total dedication to God in this point) is understood to be one of the strongest testimonies of the moral riches of the Church and an indication of the very high view taken by the Church of the love of God.

At the same time, marriage and the sexuality lived in it are good and holy. In marriage, and open to the transmission of life, sexual pleasure is something good. As an honest expression of the marital relationship, the sexual act must be carried out according to its nature, open to life, and not artificially deprived of its effect (procreation) nor performed voluntarily in an abnormal way. On the other hand, seeking sexual pleasure is gravely immoral outside of the sphere of marriage.

Yet our disordered cultural environment or our own weakness can give rise to disorder in our conduct. If we sin, we need to recognize our fault, repent of it before God (in Confession), and use the experience to avoid having it happen again. It is important to keep up the fight. "We all know by experience," we read in *The Way*, "that we can be chaste, living vigilantly, frequenting the sacraments and stamping out the first sparks of passion before the fire can spread" (no. 124).

This means taking care in what we read, see on television, what we look at on the street. In this way, we will be freer, imposing on our conduct the order we desire. Carelessness does great harm. The passions that are part of our fallen nature are always with us; and our Lord pointed out that "everyone who looks at a woman lustfully has already committed adultery with her in his heart" (Mt 5:27).

Sometimes falls are the result of a gradual, subtle process. Someone who deals regularly with a person of the opposite sex can begin to have feelings which are more than just a friendship and signal falling in love. This is a beautiful reality which God intends for most men and women as the normal path to conjugal friendship. But it is not the path for someone with a special commitment to God or a prior commitment to a married partner. If such a person becomes aware of strong inclinations of the heart toward another, he should limit this contact, create a certain distance, try not to think of that person, go more deeply into his other loves.

Chastity is closely linked to the other virtues. Progress in them (dominating laziness, being more sober, more demanding on oneself in one's work, etc.) will have an impact here and vice versa. In a special way, humility helps one to live chastity well, while the contrary vice, pride, leads to disorders in this matter also. Humility also helps a person to rectify mistakes and to be sincere with himself, recognizing that there may have been complicity in some cases. It is essential also to be sincere with one's confessor or spiritual director, disclosing the difficulties one experiences in this matter despite the feelings of shame this causes. These means, along with true devotion to our Lady, will enable one to live chastity well.

Chastity, which Christian tradition also calls purity, gives human beings a great capacity to love; it makes them strong and pleasing in God's eyes. "What God asks of you is that you should sanctify yourselves, and keep clear of fornication. Each of you must learn to control his own body, as something holy and held in honor, not yielding to the promptings of passion, as the heathen do in their ignorance of God" (1 Thess 4:3–5 [Knox trans.]). Someone who tries to live this way will experience the truth of the Lord's promise: "Blessed are the pure in heart, for they shall see God" (Mt 5:8).

7.

Humility

St. Mark has preserved a delightful scene of Christ with his disciples. "They came to Capernaum; and when he was in the house he asked them, 'What were you discussing on the way?' But they were silent; for on the way they had discussed with one another who was the greatest" (Mk 9:33–34). Wanting to give them a lesson, Jesus set a child before them. "Truly, I say to you, unless you turn and become like children, you will never enter the kingdom of heaven. Whoever humbles himself like this child, he is the greatest in the kingdom of heaven" (Mt 18:3–4).

How human are ambition and egoism—and always accompanied by the same thing: discord, quarrels, rancor. As the Book of Proverbs says, "By insolence the heedless make strife" (13:10).

Pride is the origin of almost all human ills, the vice that most threatens each person and society. It consists in a disordered love of oneself, or, as St. Thomas Aquinas expresses it, "the disordered appetite for one's own excellence" (*S. Th.*, II–II, q. 162, a. 2, c.). It is disordered love in that one ends up loving oneself more than one deserves and considers oneself better than one really is. At the heart of pride is a lie about oneself.

Everyone tends to pay much attention to his good qualities and overlook his defects. And this exaggerated self-esteem tends to grow. One can lose all capacity for self-criticism and become absurd. There is something grotesque about a person overly proud of his looks, the cost of his home, his knowledge. Other people have little toleration for vanity.

Vanity is a ridiculous eagerness to display what one considers valuable in himself. The vain man may even practice hypocrisy, feigning to be richer, wiser, more able, or a better sportsman than he is. In the end the hypocrite has trouble telling what is real from what he has invented.

Self-love is caused by lack of attention to others. The proud person is centered on his own things; all his energy goes to satisfying his ambitions or caprices. He is an egoist, an antisocial being. When with others, he tends to speak about himself—even his own illnesses or dreams if he has nothing else to say—and to demand attention. Sometimes, he even provokes attention artificially. He is inclined to judge others harshly, and whatever he says about them involves an implicit comparison with himself. Usually, therefore, he is highly critical of those who surpass him in any way and he is contemptuous and cruel regarding those he considers inferior. His comparisons give rise to envy, anxiety, rancor, and sometimes base actions directed at undercutting those who get ahead of him.

Such a person is very sensitive to the judgments of others. He begs for flattery and does not forgive criticism. Everything becomes a pretext for giving insults and taking offense. This creates an endless spiral of complications. If people don't make a fuss over him, he complains that they don't care about him; if they do, he takes it for hypocrisy or mockery.

One who loves himself a lot loves his opinion. He believes himself to be in possession of the truth and does not tolerate contradiction. He tends to take extreme positions for the pleasure of standing out. And he defends his opinions with such force that it is practically impossible to disagree. This can be very disadvantageous in scientific and academic life, for it destroys the flexibility needed to accept the opinions of others and correct one's own errors. Such people sometimes maintain a real intellectual dictatorship whose only basis is pride. But pride is a sin often found in powerful people in general.

Pride tends to subject others and resist being subjected. The proud man resists obeying; it is difficult for him to submit to a norm and do what everyone else does. If he cannot command, he wants at least to be excused from having to obey. For this reason he tends to be harsh and critical toward those who govern him. And when he has occupied important posts or considers himself invested with some authority based on past merits, his tendency to stand apart and rebel becomes more acute. St. Teresa says: "Be very careful about your interior thoughts, especially if they have to do with precedence. May God, by His Passion, keep us from expressing, or dwelling upon, such thoughts as these: 'But I am her senior'; 'But I am older'; 'But I have worked harder'; 'But that other sister is being better treated than I am.' If these thoughts come, you must quickly check them; if you allow yourselves to dwell on them, or introduce them into your conversation, they will spread like the plague and . . . may give rise to great abuses" (*The Way of Perfection*, 12, 4).

Pride is undoubtedly the gravest sin because it is the one that does the most damage. It profoundly weakens the capacity to relate to others and to God, which is the highest capacity of the spirit. For the spirit grows in the measure in which it gives itself in friendship and love, going out of itself to give itself to others. But pride closes the spirit in on itself. The soul diminishes within the narrow boundaries of egoism.

Pride is the vice most opposed to a right relationship with God. "The beginning of man's pride is to depart from the

Lord; his heart has forsaken his Maker" (Sir 10:12). The man who is not disposed to recognize his great need for help will find it hard to meet God.

God is very sensitive to human pride: "Pride and arrogance and the way of evil and perverted speech I hate" (Prov 8:13). On the other hand, he is inclined to love humility: "God opposes the proud, but gives grace to the humble" (1 Pet 5:5).

Humility is the basis for all the virtues. While pride is born of self-deception, humility resides in accepting the truth about oneself "I was wondering once," says St. Teresa, "why Our Lord so dearly loved this virtue of humility; and all of a sudden—without, I believe, my having previously thought of it—the following reason came into my mind: that it is because God is Sovereign Truth and to be humble is to walk in truth" (*The Interior Castle*, VI, 10).

The highest truth about man is discovered above all in the light of God: whatever good we have comes from God, while the miseries of our life are the fruit of our sins. "Self-knowledge leads us by the hand, as it were, to humility" (*The Way*, no. 609).

The humble person experiences intimately the truth of these words of St. Paul: "What have you that you did not receive? If then you received it, why do you boast as if it were not a gift?" (1 Cor 4:7).

Humility's effects are the opposite of those of pride. They lead one to center one's life on others and not on oneself. Praise makes a humble person uncomfortable, since he feels it is unmerited and outweighed by his errors. "The more I am exalted, Jesus, the more I want you to humble me in my heart, showing me what I have been, and what I will be if you leave me" (*The Way*, no. 591). The humble person does not think he deserves anything special for doing as he should; he takes to heart the words of our Lord: "When you have done all that is commanded you, say, 'We are unworthy servants; we have only done what was our duty'" (Lk 17:10). Indeed: "The day you see yourself as you are, you will think it natural to be despised by others" (*The Way*, no. 593).

A humble person values the virtues of others and learns from them. St. Teresa says: "Let us strive, then, always to look at the virtues and the good qualities which we find in others, and to keep our own grievous sins before our eyes. . . . This is a course of action which, though we may not become perfect in it all at once, will help us to acquire one great virtue—namely, to consider all others better than ourselves. *In this way we shall begin to profit, by God's help*" (*Life*, 13, 6).

Humility grows when one has a true knowledge of oneself, accepts opportunities to surrender one's own judgment and obey, follows what is prescribed and required of everyone, accepts with joy humiliations, reprimands, corrections, and insults, values the virtues and qualities of others above one's own, readily takes part in work that is not highly esteemed or is performed in more modest places, does not take oneself too seriously, is convinced that without God no one can take a single step. There is a degree of humility that we must ask for but which God gives to anyone who wants it. "Nothing but humility is of any use here," says St. Teresa, "and this is not acquired by the understanding but by a clear perception of the truth, which comprehends in one moment what could not be attained over a long period by the labor of the imagination—namely, that we are nothing and that God is infinitely great" (*The Way of Perfection*, 32:13). This is the profound humility of the Virgin Mary, expressed in the *Magnificat*: "My soul magnifies the Lord, and my spirit rejoices in God my Savior, for he has regarded the low estate of his handmaiden" (Lk 1:46–48).

The engine of Christian humility—as of all asceticism—is love of God. "Only one who truly loves," says St. Gregory the Great, "does not think about himself" (*Hom 38 super Ev.*).

St. Augustine sums it up in these famous lines: "Two cities have been formed by two loves: the earthly by the love of self, even to the contempt of God; the heavenly by the love of God, even to the contempt of self. . . . For the one seeks glory from men; but the greatest glory of the other is God, the witness of conscience. . . . In the one, the princes and the nations it subdues are ruled by the love of ruling; in the other, the princes and the subjects serve one another in love" (*The City of God*, 14:28).

8.

Simplicity

One of the most beautiful tributes spoken by our Lord is found in the Gospel of St. John: "Jesus saw Nathaniel coming to him, and said of him, 'Behold, an Israelite indeed, in whom is no guile!'" (Jn 1:47). The figure of Nathaniel (who very probably is the same person as Bartholomew) is one of the most attractive in scripture.

There was no guile in him: he had overcome the natural tendency to protect oneself from others, hiding his intentions, habits, or defects from them. His behavior and his words told what he was thinking and how he was. This undoubtedly gave him a special charm.

People tend to conceal themselves, intuitively thinking it dangerous to reveal themselves just as they are or from fear of mockery or in hopes of obtaining some advantage. At times self-concealment is due to pride or vanity, because one wants to be thought better than one is. Other times it is due to craftiness—one wishes to act without tipping one's hand. And it cuts one off from others and from God.

The lives of people dominated by this tendency becomes a charade. They create an image and live behind it. Calculation rules their behavior. Nathaniel received the highest praise of

our Lord, but hypocritical behavior received his harshest con-
demnations. Of the guile of the Pharisees he said: "Practice
and observe whatever they tell you, but not what they do; for
they preach, but do not practice. They bind heavy burdens,
hard to bear, and lay them on men's shoulders; but they themselves will not move them with their finger. They do all their
deeds to be seen by men" (Mt 23:3–5). And again: "Woe to
you, scribes and Pharisees, hypocrites! For you are like white-
washed tombs, which outwardly appear beautiful, but within
they are full of dead men's bones and all uncleanness. So you
also outwardly appear righteous to men, but within you are
full of hypocrisy and iniquity" (23: 27–28).

Our Lord shows us what the standard of our conduct
should be: "Beware of the leaven of the Pharisees, which is
hypocrisy. Nothing is covered up that will not be revealed, or
hidden that will not be known. Therefore whatever you have
said in the dark shall be heard in the light, and what you have
whispered in private rooms shall be proclaimed upon the
housetops" (Lk 12:1–3). That is, we always have to act as if
our actions could be seen by everyone.

In other words, get rid of concealment and pretense. If we
try to live honorably, there will be no need for them, and we
can show ourselves sincerely as we are. Someone who decides
to live like this understands perfectly the words of our Lord:
"The truth will make you free" (Jn 8:32)—free of constantly
calculating what will look good to others and what will look
bad. This does not mean being so simple that one goes about
blabbing private matters to anyone and everyone. It means
not having to worry about people who are close to us knowing
us as we are.

A major aspect of simplicity is sincerity, which is also a
virtue: the habit of speaking the truth, so that what we say
reflects what we think. "Let what you say be simply 'Yes' or
'No'; anything more than this comes from evil" (Mt 5:47).

Sincerity has to be the norm of our relations with others. Only to the one who asks what he does not have a right to know may we refuse an answer or reply evasively. Otherwise, we should not hide the truth.

We have to be especially sincere with our family and friends, who have a right of access to our privacy. Such communication is necessary to maintain those relationships. The people who love us have a right to know our state of mind, our troubles, our joys and concerns. Sometimes, of course, it will be otherwise for the sake of prudence: if, for example, disclosing something will make the other party very sad or he or she lacks the capacity to understand. Obviously, too, there are parts of our private life we have no reason to share, such as professional secrets. This would not be sincerity, but imprudence or verbal intemperance. But otherwise those who love us have a right to know us well.

Sincerity also should be practiced with our spiritual director or regular confessor, if we have one. Spiritual direction is founded on mutual trust: the director commits himself to give attention and help, the one receiving direction to explain with simplicity what happens to him. If shame leads him to dissemble, the relationship is vitiated and it would be better to terminate it. Pretense is absurd, like going to a tailor and standing on tiptoe to appear taller. How odd that new suit will look and how badly that customer will have cheated himself!

Naturalness in behavior, behaving in accord with what one is and thinks, is another aspect of simplicity. At times, charity may demand that one tone things down a bit; other times, courtesy made require some play acting (e.g., hiding boredom or impatience). But outside those obligations of charity or courtesy, we should behave naturally. Sin is the only thing we need to feel ashamed of—before God and at times before men. But nothing else.

A man should not feel embarrassed, for example, that his father has a humble social position or a humble job. No one should feel ashamed of the color of his skin, his race, his ancestry, his physical defects or those of family members or friends. Nor should our opinions, beliefs, customs, or work embarrass us if they are not an offense against God. It may not be necessary to proclaim them everywhere, but we have to avoid being ashamed.

We should not let ourselves be burdened by human respect. "They say" is a real tyrant that can affect our behavior more than we imagine. Especially when one is young, this "they say" has an enormous influence, and someone's sarcastic smile can move a young person to despise a part of himself.

An upright person has to act as he is and thinks, in all circumstances and surroundings. This is very important in regard to the faith. Our Lord—knowing how much we are affected by human respect—made that very clear: "Whoever is ashamed of me and of my words, of him will the Son of man be ashamed when he comes in his glory" (Lk 9:26). And: "Everyone who acknowledges me before men, the Son of man also will acknowledge before the angels of God; but he who denies me before men will be denied before the angels of God" (Lk 12:8–9).

To overcome human respect one must sometimes be hard on oneself. In a non-Christian environment, a Christian has to know how to behave as such: for example, how to get his friends or fellow workers to respect his convictions. It makes things easier to be clear from the start. "Undoubtedly your life will clash with theirs; and that contrast—faith confirmed by works!—is exactly the naturalness I ask of you" (*The Way*, no. 380). Regaining the ground one has lost through a so-called compromise may not be possible.

Our friends and companions need to know that we mean to fulfill our religious obligations (for example, attending Mass on Sundays) and to direct our conduct by Christian morality. If we make these things clear with good humor but firmness, from the beginning, it will be easier. And if that can't be done, we may need to change our friendships or seek other work. But that is an extreme case. Christians can rely on God's grace to help them to live their faith in the surroundings in which they find themselves, and also to Christianize that environment. "Children of God—like yourself—cannot be afraid of living in the professional or social surroundings which are proper to them. They are never alone! God Our Lord, who always goes with you, grants you the means to be faithful to him, and to bring others to him" (*The Forge*, no. 724).

9.

Cheerfulness

"Make a joyful noise to the Lord, all the lands! Serve the Lord with gladness! Come into his presence with singing! Know that the Lord is God! It is he that made us, and we are his; we are his people, and the sheep of his pasture. Enter his gates with thanksgiving, and his courts with praise! Give thanks to him, bless his name!" (Psalm 100). The nearness of God and the knowledge that he loves us produce joy.

Joy or cheerfulness is a natural movement of a soul that knows itself to be the possessor of goods. The joy corresponds to the goods. There is a joy in satisfying elementary needs such as the need for food or drink. There is the joy of obtaining some material good: a house, a car, payment for work, a raise. But there is no joy comparable to that of knowing oneself to be loved and understood.

The most stable, firm, faithful, and powerful love is the love of God. Joy naturally sets the tone of Christian life. "Cheerfulness is a necessary consequence of our divine filiation, of knowing that our Father God loves us with a love of predilection, that he holds us up and helps us and forgives us" (*The Forge*, no. 332). "If we feel we are beloved sons of our Heavenly Father, as indeed we are, how can we fail to be happy all the time? Think about it" (*The Forge*, no. 266).

If we are near to God, nothing can worry us. Even when we encounter disagreeable realities, it is because God wanted them for us, and so we hope to obtain some good from them. "We know that in everything God works for good with those who love him, who are called according to his purpose" (Rom 8:28).

Cheerfulness arises spontaneously from Christian life. It is an inseparable companion that helps us travel toward God, overcoming difficulties and encouraging others to follow the same path. For cheerfulness to become habitual—a virtue—one must foster it, promote what makes it grow, and avoid what causes sadness.

The natural support of cheerfulness is optimism, which consists in seeing the positive side of things. This does not mean fooling ourselves about negative realities. It means living in accord with the decision—which in a Christian is inspired by trust in God—that it is worth the effort to live cheerfully.

Optimism is illustrated in the case of the bottle that the optimist sees as half full and the pessimist sees as half empty. In the end one just has to choose, and a man or woman of God, who knows that the world is good and that God is behind things and events, should choose optimism and look at the world and history with joy. A thousand beautiful things surround us every day. We need to open our eyes and look.

We notice a tendency to sadness and discouragement when we encounter it in others. Everyone avoids the sad person who takes every opportunity to talk about his troubles. We are attracted by the cheerful person who always sees the good side of things and encourages us. A sad temperament is alienating, but a joyful temperament brings people together. There is something positive in optimism that we have to stir up.

Some individuals complain of their bad luck, but they should be more objective. "It is all too easy to say: 'I'm useless; nothing turns out right for me—for us.' Apart from not being true, that pessimism masks a great deal of laziness. There are things you do well, and things you do badly. Fill yourself with joy and hope on account of the former; and face up to the latter—without losing heart—in order to put things right; and they will work out" (*Furrow*, no. 68). The founder of Opus Dei used to recommend that someone with a feeling of failure take a close look at the facts: ordinarily, not "everything" went badly, but only "some specific points." If we consider how to improve in these areas, the situation may be saved. But if we wallow in pessimism, nothing can be done.

It is important, however, not to dwell on the ways things go wrong and especially not to let these motives of bitterness invade the time dedicated to relaxation or to family and friends. Limit the time spent thinking about failures to the time it takes to avoid repeating them.

At times, it is helpful to go more deeply into the motives for our sadness, because it is there that we need to apply a remedy. Sadness arises in the face of failed aspiration. Therefore we need to know where our heart is. Often the origin of sadness is unsatisfied pride, excessive attachment to ourselves: "You are unhappy? Think: there must be an obstacle between God and me. You will seldom be wrong" (*The Way*, no. 662). Perhaps we yearn in a disordered way for something we don't have—goods, positions, honors—and fail to value what we have. Nothing does more damage than to cultivate a discontent in regard to one's social position or work, for in such matters there is no ideal situation on this earth. "As far as states in life are concerned," writes Father Luis of Granada, "we can never finish speaking of the little happiness there is in them and the desire each has to change places with someone else, believing that there he would find more rest. And thus men act like a sick person, who keeps turning in his bed from one place to another, believing that with these turns he will find more comfort, and does not find it, because the cause of his discomfort is within himself, the sickness."

This happens because we spend too much time thinking about ourselves: fretting over the little things of life is a constant source of bitterness. The obvious remedy is to think about the others instead. "To give oneself sincerely to others is so effective that God rewards it with a humility filled with cheerfulness" (*The Forge*, no. 591). If we become accustomed to thinking more of others, nearly all our troubles will disappear, even big ones. "What really makes a person unhappy and even destroys a whole society is the frenzied search for well-being and the attempt to eliminate, at all costs, all difficulties and hardships. Life has many facets, very different situations. Some are harsh, others may seem easy. Each situation brings its own grace. Each one is a special call from God, a new opportunity to work and to give the divine testimony of charity. I would advise those who feel oppressed by a difficult situation to try to forget about their own problems a bit and concern themselves with the problems of others. If they do this they will have more peace and, above all, they will sanctify themselves" (*Conversations*, no. 97).

At times, of course, the reasons for sadness are real and serious. Pain and death are facts of life, and happiness cannot be perfect in this life. "The joy of us poor men, even when it has supernatural motives, always leaves behind some taste of bitterness. What did you expect? Here on earth, suffering is the salt of life" (*The Way*, no. 203). One must be ready to accept one's cross, which is bound to come in one way or another. If we know how to carry it in a Christian way, loving God, we will experience the joy of participating in the Cross of Christ, of helping him in the Redemption. It is as St. Paul says: "Now I rejoice in my sufferings for your sake, and in my flesh I complete what is lacking in Christ's afflictions for the sake of his body, that is, the Church" (Col 1:24). When the time comes, that will fill us with peace and give us strength to live the most difficult moments well. "Rejoice in the Lord always; again I will say, Rejoice. Let all men know your forbearance. The Lord is at hand. Have no anxiety about anything, but in everything by prayer and supplication with thanksgiving let your requests be made known to God. And the peace of God, which passes all understanding, will keep your hearts and your minds in Christ Jesus" (Phil 4:4–7).

The basis of joy is faith, its support is hope, but its origin is, as always, charity: the love that leads us to be concerned about God and others.

10.

Prudence

Human beings possess the ability to make free, self-determining choices. Rather than being at the mercy of external stimuli, people have an interior space where they make their own decisions. That interior space is the guarantee of human freedom. It gives human behavior its characteristic depth and dignity.

But it is necessary to nurture and protect the interior space. Children scarcely have it, and so they are scarcely able truly to exercise their freedom. If they are hungry, they eat; if they can't eat, they cry. Their comportment is superficial. As maturity develops, a true capacity to govern oneself begins to appear. And here is the area proper to the exercise of the virtue of prudence, which consists in the habit of deciding well at each moment what one has to do. To the extent one can govern oneself, one also acquires a capacity to govern other people or things.

Prudence creates the interior space and gives depth to the human person. All men have free will by nature, but not all know how to use it well. Some resemble those old player pianos that rattled through a set number of pieces when their machinery was set in motion.

Some don't even realize that they are acting out a script prepared for them by someone else. They live by the rhythm of social conventions and the dictates of fashion. "What has to be done" varies from time to time, but they cannot explain why something must be done. They do what they do because everybody is doing it. Yet human beings aren't robots. Each has his own intellect and will and should be guided by them, the intellect supplying and evaluating the elements of possible action; the will making the actual choice.

A Christian is someone who knows the purpose of his life is to love God and serve others. He therefore knows the fundamental criteria that should guide his behavior and, in judging proposed courses of action, he takes direction from their source. This judgment is called conscience.

Lacking standards of judgment, one has no way of determining the right thing to do in situations of choice. Therefore, the first thing people need is formation—and, if they are Catholics, a good knowledge of the moral doctrine of the Church. Without formation, one must turn to improvisation, conjecture, and opinion. This makes clear why we need moral criteria to make our choices and actions consistent and fruitful.

Formation can't be improvised. Serious study grounded in the reading of solid literature. And for this the advice of someone who knows the field is necessary. The counsel of St. Teresa of Avila is still valid: "This is no time for believing everyone; believe only those whom you see modeling their lives on the life of Christ. . . . Believe firmly in the teaching of our Holy Mother the Roman Church. You may then be quite sure that you are on a very good road" (*The Way of Perfection*, 21, 10).

Once we have acquired the criteria that should guide a Christian life, we must put them to use in making moral decisions. For example, if I am thinking of buying a new house, I must ask myself if the expenditure is really necessary or simply a caprice. If I am thinking of changing jobs, will the change help me or hinder me in serving my family and others?

And if factors like these aren't the ones directing us, we need to consider whether our real criteria are things like pride, sensuality, laziness, and ambition. Pride has a rare ability to hide behind apparently upright motives. Laziness can always find excuses to avoid effort. Ambition is quick to see honorable reasons for pursuing riches and fame. Sensuality adopts the appearance of naturalness in seeking satisfactions. We must examine our motives in order to purify them and be sure we are deciding rightly. "If God were the sole object of our desire, we should not be disturbed so easily by opposition to our opinions. . . . Many, unawares, seek themselves in the things they do" (*The Imitation of Christ*, I, 14, 2).

Being sincere with oneself is not easy. Rarely can we avoid the influence of the passions even when trying to work for God. Especially in making big decisions, we must calm down and let him speak to us, without substituting our will—perhaps far from upright—for his.

Once we know the moral criteria that should govern our acts and are assured of the rectitude of our intentions, prudence comes into operation in deciding well. St. Thomas Aquinas (*S. Th.*, II–II, q. 47, a. 8, c) points out that a decision has three distinct parts: deliberation, in which the circumstances of the case are studied and the relevant criteria are identified; decision or judgment, in which the choice is made; and finally execution, carrying out the choice.

The period of deliberation is critical, since the other two stages depend on it. First one needs to decide what circumstances should be taken into account. Next one must bring together the criteria and knowledge that apply—or if we lack them, try to acquire them. (For example, a professional in some field—lawyer, engineer, police officer, and so on—needs sufficient knowledge to be able to resolve ordinary cases rapidly.)

Requisite information has to be acquired. It would be culpable negligence for a decision-maker to make a bad decision because he or she neglected to get information.

In important matters that greatly affect one's own life or the lives of others, it is a norm of prudence to ask for advice in order to get better perspective on the question. This is especially so when one is personally and closely involved, as in questions of vocation, family matters, work, choice of a place of residence, resolving disputes with people close to us, and so forth. Good counselors will have three characteristics: they are fond of us, competent regarding what's involved, and capable of telling us the truth.

Asking advice is indispensable in making important decisions of governance. Besides asking those who have some legitimate claim to be heard, one should consult experts and other prudent people. But the one who must make the decision must remain free to make it, and not permit advice to become coercion. Similarly, cowardice should not move the decision-maker to shift responsibility to advisors.

Loyal counselors are a treasure. They must have the freedom honestly to say what they think. People in charge who harass advisors who don't think as they do, or simply pass over them, will find themselves surrounded by flatterers and yes-men in the end.

It will be helpful, also to acquire the habit of considering important decisions in the presence of God, our best advisor.

Next comes the decision. Decisions should be made only after sufficient deliberation. This includes giving matters only the time they deserve. Wasting time on trivialities leads to rushing important decisions because there isn't enough time left.

If possible, urgent decisions often should wait—at least until the information has been assembled and one is in a composed frame of mind. "We must try to keep our peace, even if only so as to act intelligently, since the man who remains calm is able to think, to study the pros and cons, to examine judiciously the outcome of the actions he is about to undertake. He then plays his part calmly and decisively" ("Human Virtues," *Friends of God*, no. 79).

At the same time, we should be aware that laziness often leads people to put off important decisions. Nothing is gained this way. On the contrary, this negligence can harm oneself and others. But neither should one allow the best to become the enemy of the good. Someone who only decides things when conditions are perfect will accomplish very little in this life. Things should be done as well as they can, but within the limits of what is possible.

Last of all, execution: putting into effect what's been decided. It is weakness to delay for no good reason, and delaying can lead to trouble. Reconsidering a decision made should be avoided unless new data have come to light. This is the road to peace of mind, since in this way we begin things and finish them. "Don't confuse serenity with being lazy or careless, with putting off decisions or deferring the study of important matters. Serenity always goes hand in hand with diligence, which is a virtue we need in order to consider and solve outstanding problems without delay" (*The Forge*, no. 467).

Prudence is a crucial virtue. It helps us organize our conduct reasonably. It is a virtue of virtues. Prudence makes men pleasing to God and is itself a gift of God that we should ask for. "For wisdom is better than jewels, and all that you may desire cannot compare with her" (Prov 8:11).

11.

Integrity

It's said that every man has his price—pay enough and you can get anyone to do what you want, good or bad, honorable or not. But this isn't true. Although money is the central goal in the lives of many people—and they can be bought—this isn't so for others if it's a question of conscience or duty. When we encounter someone like this, we admire his or her conduct and conclude that this is a person of integrity. There has never been a lack of such people.

But people don't get to be like this automatically, like plants which grow and give fruit without knowing it. Rather, this is the result of an effort to live an upright life. Honesty or integrity is a virtue and thus the result of the repetition of good acts that leave behind a good habit.

The will by itself tends toward the good: it spontaneously loves whatever presents itself as a good. But there is an infinity of goods within our grasp, and we cannot possess all of them at the same time. It is necessary to reflect and decide which is best in each case, then do what is right even if it's not easy or conflicts with one's preferences. So, for instance, reading a good novel is something good, but it is impossible to study at the same time. Is this a time for resting or studying? To decide correctly is proper to the virtue of prudence, but to love one's duty is proper to integrity. Therefore integrity also is referred to as "strength of will." It is the virtue that strengthens the will to love one's obligations.

Prudence and integrity complement one another and are the crown of the moral life. We are capable of firmly loving what is good and ordered to our end to the extent we dominate our passions: laziness, egoism, etc. In the absence of virtues, the passions govern us.

Passions oppose the intellect's effort to judge what ought to be done by applying general moral criteria to the circumstances of each case—the judgment of conscience. An upright will loves and follows that judgment, but if it is not upright it refuses and looks for excuses. When a person is dominated by passions—ambition, laziness, sensuality, pride—they force him to act as they dictate. For example, a lazy person may see that he should do a job, but his will does not conform. He then seeks excuses, to make the judgment of intellect favor his laziness: "I'm tired," "This job is not that important," "I'll do it better tomorrow," "Someone else can do it." If he does that often enough, he grows accustomed to self-deception and acting for twisted motives.

On the other hand, the will accustoms itself to follow conscience, and over time it will come to do this with greater ease. The intellect will grow in its ability to discern right actions. Integrity will be the fruit of this progressive refinement of conscience.

The person of integrity is governed by his sense of duty. But isn't someone who behaves honorably at risk of being taken advantage of? This is base logic. Yes, sometimes there is a material benefit in not being honorable. But what makes a person happy is not material goods, but those of the spirit. Love, friendship, joy, peace of soul—these things are not for sale. Someone who lives according to his sense of duty lives in harmony with God, with others (even when they don't understand him), and with himself.

When we see this peace in someone, it attracts us spontaneously. That explains the prestige enjoyed by a person who tries to be honorable. Substitutes don't work. Integrity can't be counterfeited, and its presence gives a great consistency to one's life. Those who live with integrity inspire trust in others. People turn to them as arbiters or to give disinterested advice.

The greatest enemy of integrity is egoism, disordered love of self. There is, of course, a good love of self that leads one, for example, to take care of one's health. But egoism causes us to think ourselves more than we are and put the emphasis on satisfying our own aspirations. There is an enormous difference in the manner of life of a person of integrity and an egoist. The egoist is ruled by whims, the upright person by truth. The upright person realizes that there is more to life than his personal ambitions. The egoist imagines that the purpose of life is to benefit himself. Someone of integrity finds it easy to see life as a vocation; he is concerned with what he can give to others—to his family, to society. The egoist has a parasitic mentality that leads him to take advantage of others. Paradoxically, of course, he who gives enriches himself, while he who seeks only his own advantage is humanly impoverished.

In Sacred Scripture the man of integrity is called "just." Noah (Gen 6:9), Simeon (Lk 2:25), and St. Joseph (Mt 1:19) are all said to be just men. This scriptural understanding of justice extends to more than just economic relations. It is an interior perfection of the person, practically equivalent to holiness. Although integrity also includes justice in economic relationships, it is a broader concept.

Our strongest and most important duties are those that refer to God. They are expressed in the first three commandments of the Decalogue: "You shall love the Lord your God with all your heart, with all your mind, with all your strength. Do not take the Name of God in vain. Keep holy the Lord's day." The first commandment expresses the focal point of life and the basis of everything said in this book. The second and third express the veneration and respect we should have for God.

As we get closer to God, we feel inclined to speak to him with greater affection, but also with greater respect. Trust grows along with veneration. We perceive that we have duties toward him while he—our Creator and Father—has rights over us: to our dedication, affection, respect, and self-surrender. We can ask him for things like children, but we cannot demand that he give them. Upright people treat with sensitivity everything that has to do with God: his holy name, objects and places of worship associated with him, consecrated persons, the liturgy. They are hurt by anything—in the conduct of others or their own conduct—that might manifest a lack of refinement in these matters.

The third commandment—sanctifying the Lord's day—refers to the duty to worship God. It is a joyful duty. Catholics have a privileged way of praising God—through liturgical ceremonies, through the celebration of the sacraments, and particularly the Eucharist. But God should be praised and honored in all our actions, especially for the benefits we've received but so often take for granted.

After duties that refer to God come those grounded in family relationships: with parents, spouse, and children. Once they exist, they cannot be destroyed, not even by ingratitude or hostility. Small annoyances and misunderstandings are inevitable in close relationships. We naturally get angry more often at the people we have most contact with, but these are precisely the ones to whom we should devote the most care and attention. "Whoever honors his father atones for sins, and whoever glorifies his mother is like one who lays up treasure. . . . O son, help your father in his old age, and do not grieve him as long as he lives; even if he is lacking in understanding, show forbearance; in all your strength do not despise him. For kindness to a father will not be forgotten, and against your sins it will be credited to you. . . . Whoever forsakes his father is like a blasphemer, and whoever angers his mother is cursed by the Lord" (Sir 3:3–16).

People of integrity should have a strong social conscience and be eager to contribute to the common good. They seek the good of all, not just their own advantage or that of their group. This sense of solidarity—of responsibility for the common good—ought to extend from one's social relationships with friends to the level of the nation and beyond, from helping to wash up after a meal to paying one's taxes.

Integrity moves a person to undertake many tasks for the benefit of others. Many unjust situations in the world are of enormous dimensions and extreme complexity. A single individual cannot solve them, but that is not an excuse for indifference. And although one person may not be able to resolve the problems of a nation or a community, he or she may be able to attend to the need of one particular person who just now, on this day, comes his or her way.

Gratitude is linked to integrity. Upright people are thankful for the real service that so many people give them. That includes parents, who transmit the priceless gift of life and provide education and care for years, and teachers who have contributed to their formation. Adults sacrifice themselves to form the young. Part of the gratitude of the younger generation should go into doing for those who follow them what has been done for them.

We also have to be grateful to the many people who serve us every day in our workplace or home, in commerce or public service. Their service is not just merchandise that we can buy. Behind every service is a person whose labor ought to be more dignified, more attractive, and more bearable thanks to us.

Fidelity, the firm habit of remaining faithful to commitments, is part of being upright. We should be men or women of our word. Sometimes this is matter of formal agreement—a contract, a solemn promise. Other times the commitment is not expressed but taken for granted, as in a friendship. Each friend knows it would be a betrayal of friendship to speak badly of the other, not to stick up for him, reveal his secrets, refuse him help at a bad moment, avoid his company, or be ashamed of being known as his friend.

Something similar is true of that special friendship called engagement. Here two people feel themselves bound in a special way and know they are not free to share their affection indiscriminately with others. There is a certain exclusivity that later may be sanctioned by marriage. In that case, the exclusivity takes on a firm and definitive character. These two give each other in a solemn way the aspect of their affectivity related to conjugal life. They will remain mutually obligated until death separates them. They no longer belong to themselves and cannot freely dispose of themselves. They have a duty to share life in common.

To be a man or woman of one's word is a profound expression of human dignity.

12.

Living for Others

The natural sign that one's love for God is growing is love for others, expressed in the desire to serve them. "If any one says, 'I love God,' and hates his brother, he is a liar, for he who does not love his brother whom he has seen, cannot love God whom he has not seen. And this commandment we have from him, that he who loves God should love his brother also" (1 Jn 20–21). God has not placed us in the world alone. He has surrounded us with others, each for us an image of God. Says St. Augustine: "Just think that you, who still have not seen God, will be worthy to contemplate him if you love your neighbor, because loving your neighbor purifies your gaze so that your eyes can contemplate God" (*Treatise on the Gospel of St. John*, 17, 7–9).

Directing one's life to the service of others is crucial. "Whoever would be great among you . . . must be slave of all" (Mk 10:43). This is how one imitates Jesus Christ, who said of himself: "I am among you as one who serves" (Lk 22:27). It demands suppressing one's egotistical impulses, the desire for comfort and sensuality, and placing one's talents at the service of others.

Then one must use one's freedom in the effort to impose this rule of conduct on oneself. "Forget about yourself. May your ambition be to live for your brothers alone, for souls, for the Church; in a word, for God" (*Furrow*, no. 630). In choosing a profession and organizing one's life, service to others becomes the fundamental yardstick.

And then life becomes filled with interest and joy. The small causes of sadness arising from excessive love and concern for oneself disappear. "Would you like to know a secret to happiness? Give yourself to others and serve them, without waiting to be thanked" (*The Forge*, no. 368).

But how is one to realize this ideal? The first step is to have a disposition open toward all men and women, a universal heart, based on the knowledge that we are all children of God, brothers and sisters possessing a fundamental equality. Secondary considerations of race, color, culture, work, or social position confer no right to look down on anyone. "A son of God cannot entertain class prejudice, for he is interested in the problems of all men. . . . There is only one race of men, the race of the children of God" (*Furrow*, no. 303).

Thinking and acting like this can be hard. One may be repelled by another's habits, way of dressing, line of work, manner of speech. But he is still our brother, and one must struggle to see the child of God in this visibly defective human. "If you love only the good qualities you see in others—if you do not know how to be understanding, to make allowances for them and forgive them—you are an egoist" (*The Forge*, no. 954).

Certain ways of acting flow from this. One despises no one. One strives to mistreat no one. One tries not to judge others harshly. "Let us be slow to judge. Each one sees things from his own point of view, as his mind, with all its limitations, tells him, and through eyes that are often dimmed and clouded by passion" (*The Way*, no. 451). And one must always be ready to forgive, especially if the other person has apologized for injuring us. In all this, one must follow the counsel of St. Paul: "Love is patient and kind; love is not jealous or boastful; it is not arrogant or rude. Love does not insist on its own way; it is not irritable or resentful; it does not rejoice at wrong, but rejoices in the right. Love bears all things, believes all things, hopes all things, endures all things" (1 Cor 13:4–7).

Growing in a spirit of service involves a number of steps. The Gospels repeat the principle of equity that regulated human relations in antiquity: "an eye for an eye and a tooth for a tooth." In its time, this was a principle of moderation from which we can still learn something valuable. But our Lord went far beyond it: "You have heard that it was said, 'An eye for an eye and a tooth for a tooth.' But I say to you, Do not resist one who is evil. But if any one strikes you on the right cheek, turn to him the other also; and if any one would sue you and take your coat, let him have your cloak as well; and if any one forces you to go one mile, go with him two miles. Give to him who begs from you, and do not refuse him who would borrow from you. You have heard that it was said, 'You shall love your neighbor and hate your enemy.' But I say to you, Love your enemies and pray for those who persecute you, so that you may be sons of your Father who is in heaven; for he makes his sun rise on the evil and on the good, and sends rain on the just and on the unjust. For if you love those who love you, what reward have you? . . . You, therefore, must be perfect, as your heavenly Father is perfect" (Mt 5:38–48).

A further step is the love of neighbor God asks of his people: "Love your neighbor as yourself" (Lev 19:18; Mk 12:31). This great principle, elevated as it is, has an immediate practical application: "So whatever you wish that men would do to you, do so to them; for this is the law and the prophets" (Mt 7:12).

How sensitive we are to whatever refers to us! But when something pleases or offends us, instead of thinking of ourselves, we should think: I need to do this for others, I need to avoid that other thing. Everyone knows how important it is to feel loved, to receive attention, to be listened to. And everyone knows the pain that scorn, mistrust, misjudgment, and indifference can inflict. Knowing our own interior world well gives us the wisdom to deal with others. The practice of putting ourselves in the other person's place should become a habit, for understanding is usually the highest manifestation of charity. Even when the problem has no solution, to be understood by another helps.

Putting oneself in the place of others is also the key to living compassion. Compassion means being moved by suffering, sadness, abandonment, and any other human misery. "Blessed are the merciful, for they shall obtain mercy" (Mt 5:7).

The spirit of service must be specific. Loving one's neighbor must begin with loving those closest to us, those who share life with us: our family. This means loving not just when love comes easily—the love of young spouses, the love of small children—but also when one "doesn't feel anything." The proof of love is sacrifice. We know we truly love others when we can sacrifice ourselves for them, serve them, help them, make life more pleasant for them, with no compensation. In a family, people who cannot take care of themselves or cannot respond to love must often be served out of love: children, the sick, the aged, those going through bad stretches and unable to react to love—or even reacting negatively. Self-sacrifice is the fuel one must burn to keep a home warm.

After family, one must love friends and all those with whom one has some relationship. The obligation to wish them well and help them is greater the closer they are to us: neighbors, fellow workers, and so on.

Finally, it is necessary to love and serve people who simply cross one's path. When a doctor of the law asked, "Who is my neighbor?" Our Lord answered with the parable of the Good Samaritan. For the Samaritan, the injured Jew he encountered was his neighbor: someone to love, serve, care for. Throughout life, we also meet persons who need us. Each is our neighbor at that moment.

Getting close to sorrow, sickness, poverty, and loneliness is always a good experience that makes one think about one's way of living. The result can be a life that is more temperate, more detached; we may value what we have received from God more highly and feel a responsibility to use it better. Here is a great antidote against egoism and frivolity.

Life is short, and no one can give direct service to the world's billions of people. But we can live charity with all those who are our neighbors. And with the thousands whom one encounters in the course of a life it is possible at least to try to live the social virtues that make life more agreeable. These norms of conduct and courtesy, the fruit of the experience of centuries, express respect and consideration toward others. Giving up one's seat to an elderly or infirm person or a mother with small children, being friendly, asking for things in a refined way, and thanking people for what they do—these small gestures matter.

This way of acting makes life more agreeable to all who encounter us. The key, to repeat, is seeing everyone as a child of God. "This brief commandment has been given to you once and for all," says St. Augustine, "love and do what you like; if you are quiet, be quiet for love; if you speak, speak for love; if you correct, correct for love; if you forgive, forgive for love, have the root of love in the depth of your heart: from this root there can only come what is good" (*Commentary on the First Epistle of St. John*, 7, 9).

13.

Work

Our culture encourages people to think a lot about making good use of time. People try to multiply their activities, working feverishly and multitasking. Some are moved by the need to make a living, others by the passion for positions and riches, others by a desire for their own fulfillment. Meanwhile, still other people try to work as little as possible and avoid anything they find irksome. They love free time though they don't know how to use it and are bored. They seek to escape reality, with no intention of improving it. Probably most people fall between these two extremes.

There is an obvious fact that applies to them all. As St. Augustine puts it: "Our whole life is nothing but a race towards death" (*The City of God*, 13, 10). So what really is the meaning of life? For some, it is all that frenetic activity, which will come to an end; for others, it is killing time, even though there is so much to be done for others. Everyone needs to pray with the psalmist: "So teach us to number our days that we may acquire a wise heart" (Ps 90:12).

The greater part of the time and energy of a mature person is devoted to professional work. This is a noble reality, desired by God. From the beginning God created man "to work" (cf. Gen 2:15). "Work is man's original vocation. It is a blessing from God, and those who consider it a punishment are sadly mistaken. The Lord, who is the best of fathers, placed the first man in Paradise *ut operaretur*, so that he would work" (*Furrow*, no. 482). True, as a result of sin that reality has become something difficult—"In the sweat of your face you shall eat bread" (Gen 3:19). But it remains a noble reality.

We obtain our sustenance, contribute to society, and serve others by working. Work develops our personalities and obliges us to acquire virtues. It teaches us to concentrate, schools us in obedience, and is the matrix of social relationships.

Moreover, these natural qualities of work are ennobled by its Christian meaning. For a Christian, work is an occasion to love God, serve one's neighbor, and collaborate in the divine tasks of the creation and redemption of the world: creation, because God showed his intention to make man a cooperator when he gave him the task of dominating the earth (Gen 1:28) and caring for it (Gen 2:15); redemption, since the fulfillment of our obligations often is an opportunity to associate oneself with the sufferings of Christ, bearing—as St. Paul said—"what is lacking in Christ's afflictions for the sake of his body, that is, the Church" (Col 1:24).

This Christian meaning of work must be kept in mind in order to give direction to what we do, preserving us from useless activism and wasting time alike. Usually it is a matter of doing what we already do with a new mentality.

To encounter and love God in work requires striving to be aware of his presence. It is useful to offer up work when starting and finishing, and to raise one's heart to God with little prayers of petition and acts of thanksgiving—aspirations along the way. Reminders, like a crucifix or an image of Our Lady on one's desk, can help. Offering suggestions of this kind back in the fifth century, St. John Chrysostom said: "A woman occupied in the kitchen or in sewing a piece of cloth can always elevate her thoughts to heaven and invoke our Lord with fervor. One who goes to the market or is traveling alone can easily pray with attention. Another who is in his wine cellar, occupied in sewing the wineskins, is free to raise his soul to the Master. The servant, if he cannot go to Church because he has to go to the market to make purchases or is in other occupations, or in the kitchen, can always pray with attention and with ardor. No place is indecorous for God" (*Homily on the Prophetess Anna*, 4, 6).

Intellectual work can present special difficulties, but it too should be done with a Christian mentality. Lawyers, politicians, teachers, journalists, professors, writers, scientists, and so forth should understand the relevance of doctrinal principles to their work. Christianity does not consist of a few pious practices; by reading and study one should seek to live the very essence of one's work in a Christian way.

Work is a privileged opportunity for serving. Often, of course, one must work to support oneself and one's family. But one's work is not a mere commodity for sale. It is service to others, and that spirit of service ennobles it, whether one is a businessman or a production line worker.

The sense of service is especially important in performing public tasks. The fundamental criterion of honesty in this sphere is the common good. This is true for public servants at all levels and of all ranks. Without the sense of service to the common good, they are at risk of giving in to self-seeking and even dishonesty.

People deciding what their future profession will be should approach the question with this orientation to service. That is especially the case with students, at least many of them, who enjoy the privilege of vocational choice (for most people, that was not always so in the past). Service to others should be a central element in their decision.

The sense of service also illuminates the obligation to study. Students have the good fortune of being able to study, thanks to the support of their families and/or society. On the depth and seriousness of their study, including the habits of work they develop, depends the service that they later perform.

Most people beyond the student stage who work are engaged in normal, ordinary activities with nothing notable or important about them. Some are happy with this, others simply accept it, and still others dislike their work. It is very important that, in these routine and not particularly brilliant circumstances, one discover the Christian meaning of work.

God values any legitimate activity in which men and women engage. "Before God, no occupation is in itself great or small. Everything gains the value of the Love with which it is done" (*Furrow*, no. 487). In fact, those closest to God did not do work of a remarkable kind. St. Joseph was a carpenter; the Virgin Mary labored in domestic tasks in an unimport- ant village of Israel; our Lord himself spent many years—the greater part of his life on earth—at manual work and was known as "the artisan, the son of Mary" (Mk 6:3).

It is not Christian, then, to look down on any kind of work. All work is an opportunity to serve others and meet God. The Christian sense of a call to holiness gives dignity and charm to all tasks. "You are writing to me in the kitchen, by the stove. It is early afternoon. It is cold. By your side, your younger sister—the last one to discover the divine folly of liv- ing her Christian vocation to the full—is peeling potatoes. To all appearances—you think—her work is the same as before. And yet, what a difference there is!—It is true: before she *only* peeled potatoes, now, she is sanctifying herself peeling pota- toes" (*Furrow*, no. 498).

All jobs can be offered to God. But they must be done well. One cannot offer to God the sacrifice of Cain who gave the bad fruit of his fields: this is not an offering but a mockery.

In the first place, to work well requires learning and profes- sional competence. One must gather the necessary theoretical knowledge and then make intelligent use of one's practical experience with the aim of improving.

It is necessary, too, to make use of a set of virtues that makes work efficient. The first is punctuality, which includes not postponing what we don't like, not preferring what we do like, and doing what is most important first. In general, it is best to bring one thing to completion before going on to something else. One should not succumb to tedium, but should persevere to the last details.

Another rule is to work with order. Regularly doing things in the same way creates habits that make work easier and more effective. Order is necessary in planning a task and organizing the daily schedule as well as in physical arrangements: each thing in its place.

Work done like this for love of God is an encounter with him.

Part Two

MYSTERIES

We know that in everything God works for good with those who love him, who are called according to his purpose. For those whom he foreknew he also predestined to be conformed to the image of his Son.

— Rom 8:28–29

This second part of the book concerns aspects of the spiritual life more closely related to the action of God's grace. The first chapter deals with the central mystery of grace, the presence in us of the Holy Spirit and "Identification with Christ." From this arises the way of living described in the next chapter, "Love of God."

"Prayer" takes up the ordinary, filial relationship of the Christian with God. "The Eucharist" focuses on the central mystery of the order of things established by God in the world after sin. In the light of Christ's sacrifice we discover a true "Sense of Sin." And this leads us to be sorry and to show repentance in sacramental "Confession." The chapter called "Death and Life" discusses identification with Christ and voluntary mortification, which purifies us from the consequences of sin and shows our love for God. "Love for the Church" is a consequence of loving Christ and of knowing that redemption reaches us through it. "Christian Maturity" deals with active participation in the mission of the Church. Finally, as part of identification with Christ, one discovers "Mary, the Mother of God," who is also our mother and a sure way to Christ.

14.

Identification with Christ

Up to now we've talked about things requiring our efforts. True, even to take those steps we need to ask for God's help. Still, advancing or failing to advance in these matters—courage, detachment, chastity, spirit of service, etc.—depends a great deal on our initiative.

There is, however, a very large part of the Christian life in which the initiative is entirely God's: God acts freely in the soul as the soul strives to be more and more faithful. It is not possible to speak altogether clearly about these matters because God's mysteries are beyond the comprehension of the human intellect. In revealing them, God used images that both disclose and conceal. More important than understanding them, however, is to begin to live them. And this is something even people who are not highly educated can do, since it is God's work in the end.

One of those realities, the most important and most beautiful, is that someone who approaches God develops a likeness to Jesus Christ, to the point of becoming identified with him. This mystery is revealed in Scripture.

While traveling toward Jerusalem with his disciples, Jesus passed through Samaria. Our Lord, "wearied as he was with his journey, sat down beside the well. It was about the sixth hour" (Jn 4:6). A Samaritan woman came there to fill her water jug and a remarkable encounter took place in which Jesus brought about her conversion. Here, we consider only certain mysterious words that our Lord spoke: "Whoever drinks of the water that I shall give him will never thirst; the water that I shall give him will become in him a spring of water welling up to eternal life" (Jn 4:14). This has a parallel in Jesus' conversation with Nicodemus, an important Pharisee who came to see him at night (Jn 3:1): "Unless one is born of water and the Spirit, he cannot enter the kingdom of God" (Jn 3:5). The same relationship, between water and the Spirit, is declared also by St. John the Baptist: "I baptize you with water for repentance, but he who is coming after me is mightier than I, whose sandals I am not worthy to carry; he will baptize you with the Holy Spirit" (Mt 3:11); for it had been revealed to John that Christ was he who "baptizes with the Holy Spirit" (Jn 1:33).

The mystery of the waters and the Holy Spirit is finally clarified in Jerusalem, on the last day of the feast of Tabernacles, involving rites in which water was used to recall the exodus of Israel through the desert and to ask for rain. "On the last day of the feast, the great day, Jesus stood up and proclaimed, 'If any one thirst, let him come to me and drink. He who believes in me, as the Scripture has said, "Out of his heart shall flow rivers of living water"' (Jn 7:37–38). And the evangelist adds: "Now this he said about the Spirit, which those who believed in him were to receive" (Jn 7:39).

The Holy Spirit is, as it were, the water of the Spirit flowing into the soul of one cleansed with the waters of Baptism. This interior presence of the Spirit gives the Christian a marvelous dignity. "We are the temple of the living God" (1 Cor 6:16). "Do you not know that your body is a temple of the Holy Spirit within you, which you have from God? You are not your own (1 Cor 6:19). "The Spirit of God dwells in you"

(Rom 8:9, 11). "Do you not know that you are God's temple and that God's Spirit dwells in you?" (1 Cor 3:16).

The life of the Spirit produces a very special effect: "For all who are led by the Spirit of God are sons of God. For you did not receive the spirit of slavery to fall back into fear, but you have received the spirit of sonship. When we cry, 'Abba! Father!' it is the Spirit himself bearing witness with our spirit that we are children of God" (Rom 8:14–16).

We can call God "Father" because we have the Spirit of his Son; by this we are in some way assimilated and transformed into Jesus: "For those whom he foreknew he also predestined to be conformed to the image of his Son, in order that he might be the first-born among many brethren" (Rom 8:29). While that participation will only become perfect in heaven (Col 1:18), here on earth it is shown in a progressive identification with him. "For to me," says St. Paul "to live is Christ" (Phil 1:21); and again: "It is no longer I who live, but Christ who lives in me; and the life I now live in the flesh I live by faith in the Son of God" (Gal 2:20). Now we are no longer strangers and sojourners, "but . . . fellow citizens with the saints and members of the household of God" (Eph 2:19). One is "no longer a slave but a son, and if a son then an heir" (Gal 4:7).

In this way the messianic name of Christ is revealed in its fullness: Emmanuel, God with us (Is 7:14)—not only because he once lived on earth, but because he remains within us as well as present in the Eucharist. In his prayer at the Last Supper, Jesus promised as much: "If a man loves me, he will keep my word, and my Father will love him, and we will come to him and make our home with him" (Jn 14:23).

The presence of the Holy Spirit in one's soul also means that one participate in some way in the intimate life of God. St. Peter says: "He has granted to us his precious and very great promises, that through these you may . . . become partakers of the divine nature" (2 Pet 1:4).

God's life in us is shown by means of the action of the Holy Spirit, and this effect of the action of God is called grace. Grace makes us like Christ and introduces us into the life of the Trinity. All this is a gift of God, which is what the word *grace* means.

Likeness to Christ grows little by little, to the degree we correspond to God's invitations. The action of the Spirit in the soul leads one to get to know God better (faith), to trust in him (hope), and to love him (charity), while also loving others for him. Little by little the image of Christ appears more clearly, manifested in our living as Christ would have lived if he had found himself in our place and circumstances.

Jesus' entire life is mirrored in us, but especially his Passion, death, and resurrection. Each of the sacraments—channels of grace and of the action of the Holy Spirit—reinforces and supports this identification.

Baptism is first. The symbolic washing of the baptized person's body in the water signifies and carries out the forgiveness of sins through the death and resurrection of Christ. "Do you not know that all of us who have been baptized into Christ Jesus were baptized into his death? We were buried therefore with him by baptism into death, so that as Christ was raised from the dead by the glory of the Father, we too might walk in newness of life" (Rom 6:3–4).

Identification with Christ will reach its fullness in heaven when he "will change our lowly body to be like his glorious body" (Phil 3:21). Meanwhile, in this life, the identification grows, both because of the mysterious action of grace and because of our conscious efforts to identify with Christ. He asked us to act in this way: "Learn from me, for I am gentle and lowly of heart" (Mt 11:29). And after washing the feet of the apostles at the Last Supper, he said to them: "I have given you an example, that you also should do as I have done to you" (Jn 13:15).

The whole of Christian life consists in this imitating Jesus. In this way we recover the character of "the image of God" in which we are created (Gen 1:27). St. Paul explained this in detail to the Ephesians: "Put off our old nature which belongs to your former manner of life and is corrupt through deceitful lusts, and be renewed in the spirit of your minds, and put on the new nature, created after the likeness of God in true righteousness and holiness" (Eph 4:22–24). They were to avoid falsehood, fraud, impurity, rudeness: "Let all bitterness and wrath and anger and clamor and slander be put away from you, with all malice, and be kind to one another, tenderhearted, forgiving one another" (Eph 4:31–32). And to the Colossians he said: "You have put off the old nature with its practices and have put on the new nature, which is being renewed in knowledge after the image of its creator. . . . Christ is all, and in all. Put on then, as God's chosen ones, holy and beloved, compassion, kindness, lowliness, meekness, and patience, forbearing one another and, if one has a complaint against another, forgiving each other; as the Lord has forgiven you, so you also must forgive. And above all these put on love, which binds everything together in perfect harmony. And let the peace of Christ rule in your hearts" (Col 3:1–15).

By means of the ascetical struggle we acquire the features of Christ. Words of St. John the Baptist can be applied to this: "He must increase, but I must decrease" (Jn 3:30). Our Lord seems to refer to this work of substitution when he asks his disciples to "give up their life for love of him" (Mk 10:38; Mk 8:34; Lk 9:23, 14:27; 17:23; Jn 12:25). This means abandoning one's own loves, interests, goals, to follow Jesus, living like him, suffering with him, and identifying with him.

It would be a mistake, however, to imagine that this implies abandoning one's own personality. On the contrary, there is nothing greater or more human than to resemble the most perfect man who has ever lived on earth. The clearest testimony that identification with Christ leads to plenitude is the immense happiness that accompanies it.

Christ is for us "the door" through which to pass into the life of God (Jn 10:7), he is "the Way, the Truth, and the Life" (Jn 14:6). Our Lord expressed this by the parable of the vine and the branches: "Abide in me, and I in you. As the branch cannot bear fruit by itself, unless it abides in the vine, neither can you, unless you abide in me. I am the vine, you are the branches. He who abides in me, and I in him, he it is that bears much fruit, for apart from me you can do nothing" (Jn 15:4–5). It is impossible to take even a single step in the Christian life apart from Christ.

Part of the effort to live like Christ resides in getting to know him deeply. For this, one must meditate frequently on the Gospels, where his life, his words, his gestures can be seen. It is necessary also to speak to him directly and ask him to show us what he wants of us. "We must accompany him so closely that we come to live with him, like the first Twelve did; so closely, that we become identified with him. Soon we will be able to say, provided we haven't put obstacles in the way of grace, that we have put on, have clothed ourselves with Our Lord Jesus Christ. Our Lord is then reflected in our behavior, as in a mirror. . . . Then other people will have an opportunity of admiring him and following him" (*Friends of God*, no. 299).

From the moment someone begins identifying with Christ, love more and more becomes the motive of his or her life: love of God, as his child, and love of others for God. God himself pours his love into that person's heart so that he becomes capable of loving in that way (cf. Rom 5:5). At the Last Supper, our Lord declared his new commandment: "that you love one another; even as I have loved you, that you also love one another. By this all men will know that you are my disciples, if you have love for one another" (Jn 13:34–35).

St. John explains: "Beloved, if God so loved us, we also ought to love one another. No man has ever seen God; if we love one another, God abides in us and his love is perfected in us" (1 Jn 4:11–12).

God does not love things because they are good; he makes what he loves good. To love with God's love means not loving only those we like. It is necessary to love all mankind, including enemies (cf. Mt 5:38). And we must try to improve what we love—to make men better by bringing them to God. If this is how one must love enemies, how must one love one's brothers and sisters in the faith! Fraternal love is the highest testimony that Christ is present in Christians. But we cannot live it well without asking God to help us show his love.

St. Jerome has preserved this charming anecdote: "The blessed St. John the Evangelist, when he lived in Ephesus and was scarcely able to go to church, unless carried by his disciples, and could not say many words at a time in a loud voice, used to make only this exhortation: 'My children, love one another!' Finally, his disciples and the brethren who heard him, tired of hearing him always say the same thing, asked him: 'Master, why do you always tell us this?' And he responded with a phrase worthy of John: 'Because this is the precept of the Lord, and fulfilling it is more than enough'" (*Commentary on the Epistle to the Galatians*, 3, 6).

15.

Love of God

One of the most beautiful images Holy Scripture uses in speaking of Jesus is light. It is found in the Messianic prophecies: "The people who walked in darkness have seen a great light; those who dwelt in a land of deep darkness, on them has light shined" (Is 9:2; Mt 4:16); "I will give you as a light to the nations, that my salvation may reach to the end of the earth" (Is 49:6; Acts 13:47; Lk 2:32).

In the prologue of his Gospel, St. John speaks of Christ in these terms: "The true light that enlightens every man was coming into the world. He was in the world, and the world was made through him, yet the world knew him not. He came to his own home, and his own people received him not. But to all who received him, who believed in his name, he gave power to become children of God; who were born, not of blood nor of the will of the flesh nor of the will of man, but of God" (Jn 1:9–13). Elsewhere John repeats words he heard from Christ himself: "I am the light of the world; he who follows me will not walk in darkness, but will have the light of life" (Jn 8:12; 9:5; 12:46; 3:19).

What did Christ mean by this? He was speaking, undoubtedly, of the light of truth, which rescues intellects from the darkness of error. Not just any truth, but above all the truth about God, knowledge of God himself, who has revealed himself to us through Christ: "No one has ever seen God; the only Son, who is in the bosom of the Father, he has made him known" (Jn 1:17–18).

The image of light is a powerful symbol of the mysterious truth that comes forth from God and illumines life, not only in the order of knowledge, but also in the order of conduct. It enables one to live in a new way because it comes accompanied by grace. Thus it removes one from the darkness not only of ignorance but also of sin. Fixed in God, we can live with the dignity of children of God, "children of the light" (Eph 5:8; 1 Thess 5:5).

This light received from Christ is faith. Faith teaches us that God is a Father, that he sent his Son, and that through his Son he has made us able to participate in his life through his Spirit. Nevertheless, we do not yet know him fully, as we shall at the end of life when we "see him as he is" (1 Jn 3:2). St. Paul explains: "For now we see in a mirror dimly, but then face to face. Now I know in part; then I shall understand fully, even as I have been fully understood" (1 Cor 13:12). Faith refers to what we have not yet seen directly, but which we believe; it is "the assurance of things hoped for" (Heb 11:1). As such, it allows us to walk on this earth, following a path, without getting lost in the darkness. It teaches us who God is and what he expects of us. And since it is a gift of God, we must ask him to give it and increase it. For our part, we should try to get to know the truths of faith better, studying them and meditating on them.

Faith is enriched by the transforming action of the Holy Spirit in us. That action of the Spirit on faith has various aspects, usually referred to as the gifts of the Holy Spirit (Is 3:11). They were given in their fullness to Christ, "and from his fullness have we all received, grace upon grace" (Jn 1:16).

They include a particular penetration into the divine mysteries that leads us to understand better (the gift of understanding), sensitivity to discover in concrete cases how we should conduct ourselves (the gift of wisdom), the capacity of directing all of our knowledge of things to God (the gift of knowledge), and prudently ordering our activity and that of others (the gift of counsel).

Faith is the first step in the Christian life: believe in God and know what he expects of us, and everything else follows. To the extent one's life is illuminated by faith and the Spirit acts in one, knowledge of God grows, both theoretically and practically.

Nothing more deserves to be loved than God, but people grasp this only gradually, as the soul grows in understanding of what God is. As their moral lives improve, they acquire a greater capacity to know and to love God, and begin to glimpse what it must be like to know God face to face. And this becomes the goal of life: "Thou hast said, 'Seek ye my face.' My heart says to thee, 'Thy face, Lord, do I seek'" (Ps 27:8). St. John of the Cross says: "Any soul with authentic love cannot be satisfied until it really possesses God. Everything else not only fails to satisfy it but, as we said, increases the hunger and appetite to see him as he is" (*Spiritual Canticle*, 6, 4).

Knowledge leads to love. Upon intimately discovering the wonder of God, people find themselves inclined to love him more and more, with greater intensity. "The more one knows God in this way," says St. Catherine of Siena, "the more one loves him, and the more one loves him, the more one knows him. In this way love and knowledge mutually nourish one another" (*Dialogues*, 85). Then it is possible to speak to him as a child does, familiarly and openly, when speaking to his or her father.

In this process one discovers what it really means to say life should be spent doing God's will. One imitates Christ, who said: "My food is to do the will of him who sent me, and to accomplish his work" (Jn 4:34; 5:30; 6:38; Lk 22:52). And one comes to understand his words, "Whoever does the will of my Father in heaven is my brother, and sister, and mother" (Mt 12:50). The will of God is the foundation of such a person's life.

This is what we ask in the Our Father: "Your will be done on earth, as it is in heaven" (Mt 6:10). Someone who says this and means it no longer seeks his or her own interest but the interest of God: what serves God's plans for the peace and salvation of the world. One tries to direct everything to God, which is the most beautiful model of detachment and the most authentic sign of love for God. One begins to love the things of God more than one's own—or, better, loves them as one's own. One seeks only God's glory: "Not to us, O Lord, not to us, but to thy name give glory" (Ps 115:1). All that is not God takes second place; as St. Gregory of Nyssa says: "Anyone who has his gaze fixed solely on God is blind to everything else" (*In Canticum*, 8, 4, 9). And so one lives as our Lord urged: "Seek first his kingdom and his righteousness, and all these things shall be yours as well" (Mt 6:33).

Anyone who knows God well feels immense respect towards him and all that pertains to him. This is the "fear of God" so often mentioned in Sacred Scripture. It is a deep veneration for the divine, which grows as one comes closer to God. Among human beings, closeness often brings loss of respect, but it is just the opposite with God: the sentiment of respect for him is also called piety. In contrast, those who deal with him very little hardly seem to realize who God is.

The spirit of reverence, as has been said, extends to everything that refers to God: his Holy Name (the object of the Second Commandment), worship and the persons who carry it out, Sacred Scripture, churches, etc. Guiding it is a principle with a classic formulation: *sancta sancta tratanda*, holy things have to be treated in a holy way.

When love for God and the things of God becomes a compelling principle of action, it is called zeal. Now love freely expresses itself in all its force. Love always can and should grow. Love born to remain small is not really love, but perhaps a bit of interest or inclination or sentimentalism. Therefore zeal is intrinsically related to love of God. It leads one to put all one's energy into serving him and even to dedicate one's life to him.

All of the evangelists describe the expulsion of the merchants from the temple. Evidently the disciples were deeply impressed when our Lord, ordinarily so peaceful, "making a whip of cords . . . drove them all, with the sheep and oxen, out of the temple; and he poured out the coins of the money-changers and overturned their tables" (Jn 2:15). But only John has provided this fine detail: "His disciples remembered that it was written, 'Zeal for thy house will consume me'" (Jn 2:17; Ps 69:9). Our Lord was indignant to find God's house being treated without respect. His reaction was intended to show his disciples—and us—who God is and how he should be respected and loved.

Love of God is said to intoxicate. Raimundo Lull expresses the idea in a book about a friend (the soul) and a loved one (Jesus): "The friend went about a certain city like a madman, singing about his beloved, and people asked him if he had lost his mind. He responded that his beloved had robbed his will and that he had handed over his understanding; and that all that he had left was his memory, with which he recalled his beloved" (*Libro del Amigo y del Amado*, 54).

Love needs to express itself in tender gestures that break the daily monotony and manifest the power of love. "Crazy! Yes, I saw you in the bishop's chapel—alone, so you thought—as you left a kiss on each newly consecrated chalice and paten: so that he might find them there, when he came for the first time to those Eucharistic vessels" (*The Way*, no. 438).

Not showy displays but small, spontaneous actions in which love suddenly, unexpectedly bursts forth (a visit to the Blessed Sacrament, a little mortification, praying on one's knees for a while, saying some small crazy aspiration).

Love of God also has its shadows. God tests our love to purify it by removing the pleasure it gives us—for it is necessary to love God for himself, not because one finds it satisfying to oneself. Then things are harder: harder to talk to God, harder to be faithful to him, harder to pray, harder to fulfill one's duties. Perhaps the passions begin to stir again. Work becomes more difficult. The senses complain and one feels a general dissatisfaction.

Then it could be that God is trying to purify our love. If in spite of the dryness we try faithfully to fulfill our duties, this is a sign that we truly love God.

At such times it is important to look for support to one of the other great pillars on which the relationship with God rests: hope. It too is a gift of God. Since it lies in trusting in him, it is exercised in times of difficulty. Ordinarily these are not great misfortunes, as heavy as Christ's cross, but difficulty in conquering the passions, the natural resistance of things, and at times the resistance—sometimes natural, other times not—raised by others against what we aspire to do for God.

Hope tells us to place confidence in God: "I can do all things in him who strengthens me" (Phil 4:13). It leads to certainty that God will never abandon us: "Even the hairs of your head are all numbered" (Mt 10:30). It encourages reliance on the strength of God—"the Lord's hand is not shortened" (Is 59:1)—and leads us to think of the love of God awaiting us in heaven. This virtue is accompanied by a gift of the Holy Spirit that grows little by little: fortitude, which enables one to bear adversity and confront difficult tasks for the love of God.

At other times, dryness is not God's way of trying us but comes from one's own carelessness in dealing with him. That includes things like quitting in the face of difficulty and refusing, for want of love, to sacrifice. Eventually, growing distaste causes one to fulfill duties to God and neighbor grudgingly. This condition is called lukewarmness. It arises only after one has made some progress in the ascetical life.

Its cause is carelessness, a lack of love, which leads to negligence, to abandoning one thing after another (prayer, mortification, effort in work, the presence of God), to mistreating the things of God and to relapsing into egoism. On this slippery slope one does things poorly because they require effort, and since they are done badly, they produce dissatisfaction and repugnance. Things done at the wrong time in the wrong way, because they were delayed by laziness, become burdensome. Life grows complicated. One would like to throw it all out. And so one steadily slips down and down the slope.

The remedy is to begin again: to renew one's love. This means more forgetfulness of self; stronger dedication to work; faithfully keeping to a schedule; small, extraordinary gestures done solely for love; and the practice of examination of conscience with the aim of reconstituting the resources of the ascetical struggle. Lukewarmness is a sickness that can be overcome. The key to doing that is love of God and strong identification with Christ.

Love of God is the heart of the Christian life. Let us ask for it with strength and humility. A prayer from the twenty-first Sunday of ordinary time can help: "O God, who unites the minds and wills of your faithful, grant to your people to love what you desire, to yearn for what you promise, so that among the vicissitudes and attractions of life, our hearts may be fixed upon the joy you have prepared for us."

16.

Prayer

The Old Testament in several places says of Moses that God knew him face to face and spoke to him directly "as a man speaks to his friend" (Ex 33:11). All Christians are called to a close personal relationship with God. We are children of God, and we should have a filial relationship with him, loving and continuous. That cordial, trusting relationship is achieved by prayer.

St. Luke records that Jesus often "withdrew to the wilderness and prayed" (Lk 5:16). He did this especially before the most solemn or important moments of his public life—at its very beginning, when he spent forty days in the desert, but also habitually afterward.

To imitate Christ in his filial behavior toward God the Father, we too should dedicate time to prayer. Prayer is the path to divine intimacy. It gives maturity to Christian life. It is where desire for God is enkindled, and one learns to love him and know what he wishes. By prayer faith is nourished, hope strengthened, charity enflamed. One grows up from being an irresponsible child to being an older son or daughter who can share in the tasks and responsibilities of the paternal household.

Without prayer, one cannot advance in the things of God. "Prayer is the foundation of the spiritual edifice" (*The Way*, no. 83). St. Teresa said that "anyone who does not pray does not need the devil to tempt them"—the reason being that one cannot take a single step in the spiritual life not based on prayer: "Without this foundation every building will fall" (*The Way of Perfection*, 4, 5). It must be a fixed habit, a stable custom, for weak and inconstant prayer leads to a feeble spiritual life.

This means praying whether one feels inspired or not (since "inspiration" often depends on external things like surroundings, what we happen to have read or heard, even the working of our digestion). "Each day without fail we should devote some time specially to God, raising our minds to him, without any need for the words to come to our lips, for they are being sung in our heart. Let us give enough time to this devout practice; at a fixed hour, if possible. Before the Tabernacle, close to him who has remained there out of Love. . . . If this is not possible, we can pray anywhere because our God is ineffably present in the heart of every soul in grace" (*Friends of God*, no. 249).

Prayer should take priority. "Prayer has to come before everything. If you understand this and do not put it into practice, don't tell me that you have no time: it's simply that you do not want to pray" (*Furrow*, no. 448). This resolution must become ever stronger. Those who knew how to love God have always known this to be so.

How should we pray? The answer arises from what prayer is. "Prayer," says St. Gregory of Nyssa, "is a conversation and dialogue with God" (*Orat. I De Orat Domini*). St. Teresa writes: "Mental prayer is nothing else than a close sharing between friends; it means taking time frequently to be alone with him who we know loves us" (*Life*, 8, 2). Prayer is conversing with God about the things of our life and determination to know better the things of God's life. The founder of Opus

Dei says: "You write: 'To pray is to talk with God. But about what?' About what? About Him, about yourself: joys, sorrows, successes and failures, noble ambitions, daily worries, weaknesses! And acts of thanksgiving and petitions: and Love and reparation. In a word: to get to know him and to get to know yourself: 'to get acquainted!'" (*The Way*, no. 91).

Mental prayer—in which we try to speak alone with God—requires a certain atmosphere, the same atmosphere needed for the conversation of two people who love each other. As one can "feel" the love of the person at one's side as we walk down the street, so one should also be able to "feel" the presence of God. But to speak intimately calls for a proper setting. It will help to be in a quiet place without interruptions (a church or oratory where our Lord is present is best). Solitude and silence are required. "When you pray, go into your room and shut the door and pray to your Father who is in secret; and your Father who sees in secret will reward you" (Mt 6:6). Even more important than external silence is interior silence. "The solitude of the body is of little advantage," says St. Gregory the Great, "if there is no recollection and solitude in your heart" (*Moralia*, 30). And St. John Chrysostom adds: "When you pray, enter into your lodging. It would be good to close the doors of your quarters, but God wants something else before this, that you also close the doors of your soul" (*In Mat.*, 19, 3).

Someone who wishes to pray must withdraw attention from what he or she has been doing and concentrate on the things of God. Imagination must be controlled, to prevent it from drifting off. The hustle and bustle—often, within ourselves—and the constant interior monologue about this and that must come to a halt. "A certain quietude is a requirement of the mind," says St. Augustine. "God lets himself be seen in interior solitude" (*Commentary on the First Epistle of St. John*, 17). St. John of the Cross remarks: "Individuals who want to find him should leave all things through affection and will, enter within themselves in deepest recollection, and let all things be as though not" (*Spiritual Canticle*, 1, 6).

Then, when things are quiet, we realize that we are in the presence of God, that he loves us, that he sees what we are doing, and is interested in us and in our concerns. And now we can begin to speak.

This is not a matter of ready-made formulas or any special kind of language—only what we would use in confiding in any person who loves us. "And in praying do not heap up empty phrases as the Gentiles do" (Mt 6:7–8). Prayer should be simple and natural. "He has no wish for us to tire our brains by a great deal of talking," says St. Teresa (*The Way of Perfection*, 29, 6).

In the beginning, we will feel a need to pray for ourselves and our things. Little by little we will realize that God already knows what we need, and we will do less asking for things. Instead we will ask forgiveness for so much that we do badly; we will give him thanks, and we will praise him.

It can be a big help to use a book to center one's prayer on a theme: Sacred Scripture, especially the Psalms and the Gospels, the prayers of the liturgy, the lives of saints, books of prayer, books about the spiritual life; and also theological writings that are simple and help one know and love God. In the beginning it is useful to choose subjects with an ascetical content: the aim is to stir up love for God and see with clarity where improvement is needed. St. Teresa says, "I never dared begin to pray without a book; my soul was as much afraid to engage in prayer without one as if it were having to go and fight against a host of enemies. With this help, which was a companionship to me and a shield with which I could parry the blows of my many thoughts, I felt comforted" (*Life*, 4:7).

Read a little and, when something catches your attention, stop to consider it. Examine yourself before God in the light of what you are reading. See where you need to improve, ask God's forgiveness, make resolutions or decisions to improve. It can be a bit difficult, but prayer quickly begins to show results: you know yourself better, you know our Lord better, and you address him more seriously.

One helpful practice is the use of imagination regarding scenes of the Gospel. The founder of Opus Dei says: "First of all, imagine the scene or mystery you have chosen to help you recollect your thoughts and meditate. Next apply your mind, concentrating on the particular aspect of the Master's life you are considering—his merciful Heart, his humility, his purity, the way he fulfills his Father's Will. Then tell him what happens to you in these matters, how things are with you, what is going on in your soul. Be attentive, because he may want to point something out to you, and you will experience suggestions deep in your soul, realizing certain things and feeling his gentle reprimands" (*Friends of God*, no. 253).

Prayer is a dialogue. We begin to notice that God is asking things of us. Usually this is not some extraordinary illumination, but a growing realization leading to more refinement in some point. Little by little, we become accustomed to speaking with God about decisions we face and about what we should do to serve him better. Then, prayer becomes the motor driving our life. "A thirst for God is born in us, a longing to understand his tears, to see his smile, his face . . . The soul goes forward immersed in God, divinized: the Christian becomes a thirsty traveler who opens his mouth to the waters of the fountain" (*Friends of God*, no. 310).

Progress in prayer is not always continuous. It may seem better some days than others. It remains a struggle to control imagination, to avoid the drowsiness that can assail us—as it did the apostles (Lk 11:1)—to get rid of distractions. St. Teresa reports: "I suffered great trials in prayer, for the spirit was not master in me, but slave. I could not, therefore, shut myself up within myself (the procedure in which consisted my whole method of prayer) without at the same time shutting in a thousand vanities" (*Life*, 7, 6).

Often one finds oneself dry, not knowing what to say, with no great desire to begin or to make an effort. But prayer should not be done carelessly, for that would be a lack of refinement toward God. In these circumstances, one can use vocal prayers (the Hail Mary, the Our Father, hymns or Psalms, aspirations, etc.), repeating them very slowly and meditating on them. It may also help to use some simple book that one especially likes—the life of a saint, books of prayers. But it is not good just to read and abandon dialogue. If the cause of dryness is fatigue, this counsel of *The Way* can help: "Your mind is sluggish: you try to collect your thoughts in God's presence, but it's useless: there's a complete blank. Don't try to force yourself, and don't worry. Look: such moments are for your heart" (*The Way*, no. 102). This is the time to speak words filled with affection to God, to turn toward him in love.

Having made some progress in the ascetical struggle, one feels a need to bring to prayer the divine mysteries—the Trinity, the Redemption, the life of grace, etc.—and contemplate them. One also acquires some familiarity with those who are close to God, especially our Lady, St. Joseph, the angels. We begin to grasp something about the intimate life of God because now we begin to feel a need to live by it. "The soul is, as it were, making a discovery in the supernatural life, like a little child opening his eyes to the world about him" (*Friends of God*, no. 306).

As in human love, the conversation becomes simpler as intimacy increases. One does not feel a need to speak so much—in part, because there is nothing new to say. Those who love each other enjoy simply being together. Something similar happens in prayer. The holy Curé of Ars one day asked a good villager how he prayed; the answer was, "I look at our Lord in the Tabernacle, and he looks at me." This is the prayer of quiet and the beginning of contemplation. One is in the presence of God, loving: "Words are not needed, because the tongue cannot express itself. The intellect grows calm. One does not reason; one looks! And the soul breaks out once more into song, a new song, because it feels and knows it is under the loving gaze of God, all day long" (*Friends of God*, no. 307).

"For contemplation is a high place," writes St. John of the Cross, "where God begins to communicate and show himself to the soul in this life, but not completely. Hence he does not say that he has appeared fully but that he is in sight. However sublime may be the knowledge God gives the soul in this life, it is but like a glimpse of him from a great distance" (*Spiritual Canticle*, 13, 10). But this summit—the peak of asceticism—is not reached immediately. It takes patient effort and time, and God may still withhold it, reserving it instead for one's fulfillment in heaven. And even if God does grant this sublime knowledge to some advanced souls, John of the Cross remarks, "their experience of God in this favor is so lofty that they understand clearly that everything remains to be understood" (*Spiritual Canticle*, 7, 9).

In every case, nevertheless, prayer is the path that must be taken to reach full identification with Christ.

17.

The Eucharist

The Eucharist is, par excellence, the *Mysterium Fidei*, the Mystery of Faith. As with all of his dealings with human beings, God wished to surround this mystery with strong symbolism. It is the mystery of the Body and Blood of Christ—of the Sacrifice of Calvary and the Redemption from sin; it is also the mystery of the food of immortality and God's presence among men. All of these aspects are expressed in the symbolic actions with which Christ inaugurated it.

The central symbol is blood, the vehicle of life, which for ancient people was filled with mystery. Blood was central to the worship offered to God by the religion of Israel and many other religions, too. Worship manifests the respect that one has for God, recognizing him as Lord of all things, asking his forgiveness for sin and seeking his help. The customs of Israel recognize sacrifices of many types. But since the death of Christ on the Cross, Christianity has a single sacrifice: that of Christ.

St. John introduces this mystery by telling us that John the Baptist, upon seeing our Lord, exclaimed, "Behold, the Lamb of God, who takes away the sin of the world!" (Jn 1:29, 36). The meaning of this extraordinary expression only became clear much later, when, at the end of his public life, our Lord celebrated the Passover with his disciples. His words as reported by St. Luke express his deep emotion: "I have earnestly desired to eat this Passover with you before I suffer" (Lk 22:15).

The Passover was the greatest Jewish feast and was preceded by rites of penance and purification (Jn 11:55). The central element was a meal the evening before. This was a ritual meal, with specified blessings and prayers, psalms to sing, and food. The principal dish was the Paschal Lamb, the "Pasch," one year old and without any defect. In Jerusalem, each lamb was sacrificed in the Temple, the priests poured its blood on the altar, and people then brought it home to prepare for the meal at nightfall. The whole lamb was consumed, with nothing left over. It was not permitted to break any of its bones.

During the meal, the youngest would ask the oldest the reason for this unusual dinner. The elder would tell how God brought the people of Israel out of slavery in Egypt through great miracles, maintained them in the desert with manna, and established a covenant with them on Mt. Sinai. This covenant was sealed with the blood of a sacrifice that Moses poured on the altar and sprinkled over the people saying, "Behold the blood of the covenant which the Lord has made with you" (Ex 24:8). Part of the narrative described the calamities with which God punished the Egyptians, in particular the last in which the firstborn of all the houses of Egypt died. To save themselves from this punishment, the Israelites in Egypt painted their doorframes with the blood of the lamb of the first paschal meal as the Lord had commanded (Ex 11 and 12).

In our Lord's time, the houses of the Israelites were still marked with the blood of the lamb on this night. This is the context of the Last Supper. But there were significant variations. "When Jesus knew that his hour had come to depart out of this world to the Father, having loved his own who were in the world, he loved them to the end" (Jn 13:1). After washing the feet of his disciples, an act of courtesy usually done by servants, he announced a new commandment: "Love one another; even as I have loved you." Later in the course of the ritual meal, he instituted the Eucharist.

None of the evangelists speaks of the paschal lamb, perhaps meaning us to understand Christ himself this way; but they do speak of the blessings our Lord pronounced over the bread and the cups of wine consumed in accord with the traditional rite (Lk 22:14–20). Jesus intentionally changed two of the blessings, of the bread and of one of the cups of wine. The bread was probably that called "of the blessing," which was distributed to those present as a symbol of unity and friendship. Our Lord "took bread, and when he had given thanks, he broke it, and said, 'This is my body which is for you'" (1 Cor 11:24; Lk 22:19). "And likewise the cup after supper, saying, 'This cup which is poured out for you is the new covenant in my blood'" (Lk 22:20).

This reference to a new Covenant sealed with his own blood points to a clear parallel with the action of Moses on Mt. Sinai. Jesus evidently refers to his imminent Passion, where his body will be delivered over to the Gentiles (Mt 17:19) and his blood will be shed (Jn 19:34; 1 Jn 5:6–8). The symbolism of the Jewish Passover is thus transformed, as St. Paul implicitly notes in saying, "Christ, our Paschal Lamb, has been sacrificed."

Christ is the Paschal Lamb who, by his blood, saves us from the death of sin, as the blood of the lamb saved the firstborn among the Israelites. This is the sacrifice offered for our sins as well as the food preparing us to enter into life as the lamb prepared the Israelites to set forth into the desert. It also is the blood with which the New Covenant, the commitment between God and the people, is sealed. As in the Old Covenant, God commits himself to care for his new people, the Church, while we commit ourselves to serve him faithfully. This New Covenant gives rise to a new worship of God, as the Old gave rise to Jewish worship.

The Epistle to the Hebrews develops with great beauty the meaning of the sacrifice of Christ, comparing it with the ancient cult of Israel, which was only a shadow of what was to come (cf. Heb 9:9; 10:1). Christ is the new "high priest of the faith that we confess," and he is a holy priest. "It was fitting that we should have such a high priest, holy, blameless, unstained, separated from sinners, exalted above the heavens. He has no need, like those high priests, to offer sacrifices daily, first for his own sins and then for those of the people; he did this once for all when he offered up himself" (Heb 7:26–27). His sacrifice was in his own body (cf. Heb 10:7–10), with his own blood, not that of animals. And so: "How much more shall the blood of Christ, who through the eternal Spirit offered himself without blemish to God, purify your conscience from dead works to serve the living God" (Heb 9:14), and do this "once for all" (Heb 10:10). There is, then, a New Covenant, a new sacrifice, and a new priesthood. Here is the origin of the new worship of God, whose only sacrifice is that of Jesus on the cross and whose priesthood is a participation in the priesthood of Christ.

The Church today devoutly repeats the gestures of Christ at his Last Supper. He said, "Do this in memory of me" (Lk 22:19; 1 Cor 11:24–25) and, "As often as you eat this bread and drink the cup, you proclaim the Lord's death until he comes" (1 Cor 11:26). The Church believes firmly that these actions make really present the Body and Blood of Christ, his Passion and death on the cross.

This one Christian sacrifice is renewed mystically whenever a priest of Jesus Christ repeats his words, in his name, in the liturgical act. "The oblation itself, no matter who might be the offerer, Paul or Peter," says St. John Chrysostom, "is the same that Christ entrusted to his disciples and that his priests now carry out . . . because just as the words that God pronounced are the same as the priest says now, so the oblation is the same" (*Hom. Super Ep. 2 Tim*). Christ is still the priest and the victim of that unique sacrifice, as Origen said in the third century: "Because he who offers the sacrifice of the Father on the altar of the Cross is the same who offers his own body as victim" (*Hom. Super Gen.*, 8). St. John Chrysostom at the beginning of the fifth century declared: "It is not a man who converts the things offered into the Body and Blood of Christ, but Christ himself who was crucified for us. The priest, a figure of Christ, pronounces those words, but the power and the grace are from God. 'This is my Body,' he says. And this word transforms the things offered" (*Hom. on the betrayal of Judas*, 1).

This suggests how we should participate in the celebration of the Eucharist. It is the most sacred action performed by the Church. Here one truly renders to God the worship he deserves, recognizes his universal sovereignty, gives him thanks, asks his pardon, and asks him to help the whole Church and each of us in our needs. At the same time it is a great gesture of love of God for men.

The whole Church, those on earth and in heaven, adores God in a united way in each Eucharist, united also to the chorus of angels who praise God. The celebration begins with a petition for forgiveness of sins. Then come the reading of the word of God and its explanation in the homily, followed by the confession of faith. In the offertory, our Lord is thanked for the gifts with paschal formulas, and the bread and wine are offered, symbols of our own work, hopes, and sorrows.

The preface, a song of praise, opens the most important part, the Eucharistic liturgy. We ask help from our Lord, pray for the Church, and include our intentions. After the ancient sacrifices of Israel are recalled, the words and gestures of our Lord are repeated in the consecration. From that moment on, Christ is present on the altar, and his sacrifice is also made present. Pope Pius XII said: "Now the Eucharistic species under which He is present symbolize the actual separation of His body and blood. Thus the commemorative representation of his death, which actually took place on Calvary, is repeated in every sacrifice of the altar, seeing that Jesus Christ is symbolically shown by separate symbols to be in a state of victimhood" (Encyclical *Mediator Dei*).

At Communion, the Body of Christ is food for us. St. John reports Christ's words after the multiplication of the loaves: "I am the bread of life. Your fathers ate the manna in the wilderness, and they died. This is the bread which comes down from heaven. . . . If any one eats of this bread, he will live forever; and the bread which I shall give for the life of the world is my flesh" (Jn 6:48–51). And he added: "Unless you eat the flesh of the Son of man and drink his blood, you have no life in you; he who eats my flesh and drinks my blood has eternal life, and I will raise him up at the last day. For my flesh is food indeed, and my blood is drink indeed. He who eats my flesh and drinks my blood abides in me, and I in him" (Jn 6:53–56).

St. Paul insists on the reality of the presence of Christ: "The cup of blessing which we bless, is it not a participation in the blood of Christ? The bread which we break, is it not a participation in the body of Christ?" (1 Cor 10:16). And the Church has always taught and defended this. St. Ignatius of Antioch, around the year 107, wrote: "The Eucharist [is] the flesh of our Savior Jesus Christ, which suffered for our sins, and which the Father, of His goodness, raised up again" (*Letter to the Smyrneans*, 7, 1).

It is essential that Christ's Body and Blood be received worthily, without consciousness of mortal sin, having confessed beforehand if necessary. "Whoever, therefore, eats the bread or drinks the cup of the Lord in an unworthy manner will be guilty of profaning the body and blood of the Lord. Let a man examine himself, and so eat of the bread and drink of the cup. For anyone who eats and drinks without discerning the body eats and drinks judgment upon himself" (1 Cor 11:27–29).

Preparation is necessary to participate in Holy Mass and Communion with attention and devotion. After Mass ends, it is desirable to spend a few minutes in thanksgiving. "Do not lose" says St. Teresa, "such an excellent time for talking with Him as the hour after Communion" (*The Way of Perfection*, 34, 10).

Someone who grasps what the Eucharist is will do his or her best to attend Mass and receive Communion frequently, even daily. "If the bread is daily," St. Ambrose of Milan said at the end of the fourth century, "why do you receive it only once a year? Receive every day what is advantageous for you. Live in such a way that you are worthy of receiving him every day" (*On the Sacraments*, 5).

The saints have always exhibited great sensitivity toward the Eucharist, as in these complaints of St. Francis of Assisi: "Those who are in charge of these sacred mysteries, and especially those who are careless about their task, should realize that the chalices, corporals and altar linens where the Body and Blood of our Lord Jesus Christ are offered in sacrifice should be completely suitable. And besides, many clerics reserve the Blessed Sacrament in unsuitable places, or carry it about irreverently, or receive it unworthily, or give it to all comers without distinction. Surely we cannot be left unmoved by loving sorrow for all this; in His love, God gives Himself into our hands; we touch Him and receive Him daily into our mouths. Have we forgotten that we must fall into His hands? And so we must correct these and all other abuses. If the Body of our Lord Jesus Christ has been left abandoned somewhere contrary to all the laws, it should be removed and put in a place that is prepared properly for it" (*Letter to Priests*).

Our Lord really present in the tabernacles of our churches deserves our company. It is a marvelous custom to visit him in the tabernacle during the day. And the whole of one's Christian life should spontaneously revolve more and more around the Eucharist. Here is a prelude of eternal life. In the heavenly Jerusalem there will be no need for the sun, because the Lamb will be at its center and will illuminate everything (cf. Rev 22).

18.

The Sense of Sin

The Cross of Christ is central to Christianity. Over the centuries the Church has celebrated his death and resurrection in the Eucharist, and has united itself to Christ in offering the Father the voluntary sacrifice of the Son. Jesus of Nazareth crucified is the center of the history of salvation, which is the true meaning of human history.

The Cross is an unfathomable mystery. It is the means by which God decided to repair the sins of all men of all times and the act of reconciliation by which God forgives. "For in him all the fullness of God was pleased to dwell, and through him to reconcile to himself all things, whether on earth or in heaven, making peace by the blood of his cross" (Col 1:19–20). "In Christ God was reconciling the world to himself, not counting their trespasses against them, and entrusting to us the message of reconciliation" (2 Cor 5:19). Yet God could have forgiven us in easier ways. So why did he choose this painful way? What does he mean to say to us by the Cross?

Plainly it is eloquent testimony to God's love. "For God so loved the world that he gave his only Son" (Jn 3:16). God decided to forgive men's sins by becoming man and taking upon himself the pain and death that are consequences of sin.

Rather than leave man alone in that situation of defeat, he shared the hardest part of the human condition so that we would have company and consolation in him. "Though he was in the form of God . . . [he] emptied himself, taking the form of a servant, being born in the likeness of men. And being found in human form he humbled himself and became obedient unto death, even death on a cross" (Phil 2:6–8).

Since then, Christ is our model in all the circumstances of life, difficult as well as easy. He has given new meaning to pain, suffering, and death. "He died for all, that those who live might live no longer for themselves but for him who for their sake died and was raised" (2 Cor 5:15). Indeed, "I have been crucified with Christ; it is no longer I who live, but Christ who lives in me; and the life I now live in the flesh I live by faith in the Son of God, who loved me and gave himself for me" (Gal 2:20).

Now we can understand more profoundly the words of Christ: "If any man would come after me, let him deny himself and take up his cross and follow me" (Mt 16:24). He preceded us on the path that passes through pain and death, to his Kingdom.

But the question stands: Why did God choose to show his love for us precisely by the Cross?

The mystery of the Cross cannot be understood apart from another mystery: sin. Christian tradition speaks of a mysterious proportion between the sin of mankind and the death of Christ on the Cross. "But he was wounded for our transgressions, he was bruised for our iniquities; upon him was the chastisement that made us whole, and with his stripes we are healed" (Is 53:5). St. Paul's words are blunt to the point of being brutal: "For our sake he made him to be sin who knew no sin, so that in him we might become the righteousness of God" (2 Cor 5:21). In Christ crucified we see the sign of what human sin is. Here we shall speak of three aspects.

1. As a historical event, our Lord's death on the Cross was a result of the sins of certain particular people: the hatred and intolerance of a few scribes and Pharisees, the cowardice of those who should have defended him, the indifference of those who had reason to love him. Altogether, a relatively small cluster of human miseries combined to place the Son of God on the Cross.

Most of the men involved were not monsters of malice, nor did they have an especially intense desire to do harm. The Passion and death of our Lord were not a theater piece. Ordinary sins were enough to put our Lord on the Cross: ordinary envy, common weakness, routine cowardice, everyday indifference. Much the same thing has happened many times since. The perpetrators of atrocious crimes have often sought to excuse themselves by saying they did not know, they were carrying out orders, they were only doing what everybody else did, they meant no harm, they had good intentions, they had no choice.

We should imagine ourselves in similar circumstances and ask what we would have done. Suppose everyone said he should die; we were under a lot of pressure; people were shouting; we didn't have all the facts; Jesus really did seem kind of strange; there were good reasons to worry about what might happen. . . .

Suppose we'd been zealous Pharisees, or people in their employ, or judges used to adjusting to circumstances, or residents of Jerusalem anxious to avoid trouble, or halfhearted disciples—the bottom line would have been the same. Hatred would have led us to persecute him, or weakness to condemn him, or indifference to gaze on him with indifferent curiosity as he suffered on the cross. In the best of cases, if we were genuine disciples, we would have been scared to death and sought refuge, thinking perhaps that all those marvels experienced with our Lord might have been just a dream.

True, a few did not flee but stood by him. Mary, some other women, and John were at the foot of the Cross. But they, who loved him above all else, were alone. And if we do not love him as Mary or John did, we should not imagine ourselves standing beside them then.

God wished to dwell with humankind, and he ended on the Cross. His contemporaries put him there, but perhaps we would have done the same. God is always trying to get closer to us, seeking us in every circumstance, and frequently we reject him: when we neglect duties, allow ourselves to be carried along by our weaknesses, behave as egoists.

The Cross is a symbol of human callousness toward God. Christ's Passion is the product of all those rejections, weaknesses, indifferences, moments of cowardice. This is the primary aspect of the mystery of sin: the offense, the contempt, shown to God.

2. The Cross also expresses another profound dimension of sin: the abuse of truth. Christ is the Truth of God sent to the world (Jn 14:6)—the truth about God and about man. Those who crucified our Lord crucified the truth. Every sin is a mistreatment of the truth. In sinning one rejects the light of conscience. The truth that comes from God and is like his voice within us is ignored and rebuffed.

Sin involves deception and flight. Deception because we make what we know to be an evil choice under the guise of a disordered good, letting ourselves be deceived by false arguments. Adam and Eve, having deceived themselves and eaten of a fruit God had forbidden to them, felt it necessary to hide from God. This is the same impulse—to flee and hide—that a small child feels who knows he has acted badly. Along with trying to escape punishment, it is a flight from reality, a flight from the truth.

Many sins are sins of weakness. We act badly, not because of ill will, but because temptation overcomes us and deceives us to a certain point. Knowing we have behaved badly, we wish we had acted otherwise. We are like the disciples who really did love our Lord but, unable to overcome fear, abandoned him to death.

The light of conscience is weakened to the extent it is not followed. It is lost when one becomes accustomed to not following it. Then sin is accepted without resistance, like an old acquaintance. One can no longer say one really does not want to sin. Such a person is like one of those spectators who gazed indifferently on the Cross or like Pilate, who condemned our Lord in a spirit of skeptical blindness to the very existence of truth.

For those who add self-love to darkened conscience there is the further danger of becoming enemies of truth. This involves a strange hostility to the upright conduct of others, now viewed as a reproach to themselves. Unable to tolerate the light, they tend instinctively to persecute and punish it. In the gravest cases, they even try to destroy the foundations of upright conduct and substitute a rationale to justify their own lives. "Every one who does evil," says our Lord, "hates the light, and does not come to the light, lest his deeds should be exposed" (Jn 3:20).

This is not just weakness or blindness, but malice. It is the perversion of evil. Malice produces intolerance and aversion to the truth. There are traces of it in the mockery with which so-called friends sometimes try to humiliate one who is better; in the anger of workers not accustomed to honest work toward someone who works honestly; in the bitter rush to criticize that surges up in us when we hear praise bestowed on someone we dislike who has excelled us. Pride causes one to see what is good as in a distorting mirror. Instead of loving the good, one detests it and perceives it as an evil.

A typical manifestation of malice in its extreme form is hatred for the doctrine of the Beatitudes. This is the clearest sign of the perversion of evil. Such a person hates, without motive, the gentleness, simplicity, joy, and candor of a man or woman of God. Many persecutions can only be explained in this way. "If the world hates you, know that it has hated me before it hated you. If you were of the world, the world would love its own; but because you are not of the world, but I chose you out of the world, therefore the world hates you" (Jn 15:18).

Malice adds much to the gravity to sin. Sins of weakness separate us from God and can also be grave (sins against chastity, drunkenness, etc.); but usually they are followed at once by repentance. But when people become used to mistreating the light of God, conscience is darkened and they become indifferent. Repentance seems meaningless, and when there is repentance, it is vague and has little effect. Where there is malice, repentance becomes impossible. Goodness itself is now the enemy; and sickness of the soul expresses itself in behavior that often is pathological.

Crucified truth is the second aspect of the mystery of sin. The third aspect is the damage sin produces.

3. Human perfection supposes—because God makes it so through grace—the ability to participate in the divine life. This growth in human perfection is inseparable from a growing capacity for divine life. The full participation in God which will be attained in heaven begins on earth.

Sin damages the image of God in us, destroys the perfection of man, and makes one incapable of possessing God. Sin produces disorder in the human person, disrupts harmony, and leads to poor functioning. While right action produces joy, bad action, once the satisfaction sought passes, leaves bitterness. No longer can we love God above all things. We lose interest in seeking him and satisfaction in finding him. It is harder to reflect his life, and we become less like him.

Christ's body as it was disfigured by blows and scourging is a physical expression of how sin damages man. "His appearance was so marred, beyond human semblance. . . . He had no form or comeliness that we should look at him, and no beauty that we should desire him. He was despised and rejected by men; a man of sorrows, and acquainted with grief; and as one from whom men hide their faces he was despised, and we esteemed him not" (Is 52:14, 53:2–3). Sins mistreat and disfigure the image of God in us in a similar way.

Christ dead on the Cross is an icon of man dead through sin. Sins that cause the loss of God's life in us—the loss of the presence of the Holy Spirit and of his grace—are called grave sins, while the others are venial or lesser sins. Grave sins are also called "mortal" because they kill the life of God in us and deprive us of participating in the Kingdom God has prepared for those who love him.

While some grave sins are easy to recognize because of the observable grave damage they cause (for example, some sins of injustice), it is not always easy, since we cannot see the image of God in ourselves nor, in some cases, can we measure sins' consequences in the life of society. To help us, God has revealed the gravity of some sins. For example, St. Paul writes: "Do not be deceived; neither the immoral, nor idolaters, nor adulterers, nor the effeminate, nor sodomites, nor thieves, nor the greedy, nor drunkards, nor revilers, nor robbers will inherit the kingdom of God" (1 Cor 6:9–10).

Sin, then, is an offense against God, against the truth, and against the image of God in us. It incapacitates us to live the life of God here on earth and, after the resurrection, in heaven. For the sinner there comes a point at which, practically speaking, God signifies hardly anything for him. "The unspiritual man," says St. Paul, "does not receive the gifts of the Spirit of God, for they are folly to him, and he is not able to understand them" (1 Cor 2:14).

All of us are sinners, and we need to see to it that our hearts remain sensitive to sin instead of becoming used to what separates us from God. "If one keeps the nose of his soul healthy, he will notice how badly sin smells," says St. Augustine (*On the Psalms*, 37). And elsewhere: "Do not underestimate the faults to which you perhaps have gotten accustomed. Habit leads us to fail to appreciate the gravity of sin. What becomes hard loses its sensitivity. Whatever is in a state of putrefaction does not hurt; not because it is healthy, but because it is dead. If we are pinched at some spot and it hurts us, it means that that part is healthy and may be healed. If it does not hurt, it means that it is already dead: it has to be amputated" (*Sermon*, 17).

John the Baptist preached conversion from sin and penance as preparation for an encounter with Christ (cf. Mt 3:1). It always happens like that: meeting God requires conversion. Human life must be a story of conversions, repentances, rectifications; we see more and more clearly the things in us that obscure the image of God and we decide to get rid of them. "Imitate the sailors," St. Augustine recommends. "Their hands don't cease until they have bailed out the depths of the boat; neither do you cease to do good. Nevertheless, in spite of everything, the bottom of the ship begins to fill again, because the small cracks of human weakness are still there: and it is necessary to bail out the water again" (*Sermon*, 16).

The worst thing about sin is the offense to God. One only sees this clearly as one's Christian life advances and everything in life comes to be judged in relation to God. To obey conscience is to give him glory, to disobey is to disappoint him. Every fall, especially grave ones, is a lack of fidelity, a rejection of and offense against his love. Our faults and mistakes of conduct are not just failures of strategy or technical errors; they are offenses against God, our personal share in the tragedy of the Cross. "To sin is to crucify the Son of God, to tear his hands and feet with hammer blows, and to make his heart break" (*Furrow*, no. 993). But if we recognize our sins and struggle against them, the love of God is poured out in our hearts and fills us with his peace and his joy.

19.

Confession

"Where sin increased, grace abounded all the more" (Rom 5:20). The Cross of Christ is the guarantee of God's forgiveness. There is no sin God does not want to forgive. Repentance is the door to that forgiveness.

Our Lord came to save sinners: "Those who are well have no need of a physician, but those who are sick; I have not come to call the righteous, but sinners to repentance" (Lk 5:31–32). He explained the love that is ready to pour itself out in the parables of the lost sheep, the lost drachma, and the prodigal son, which St. Luke places together.

The first tells of a shepherd with a hundred sheep. He goes to seek the one that has gone astray, and "when he has found it, he lays it on his shoulders" (Lk 15:5). Our Lord comments: "There will be more joy in heaven over one sinner who repents than over ninety-nine righteous persons who need no repentance" (Lk 15:7). The second tells of a woman who has ten coins and loses one. After searching carefully, she finds it and is filled with joy. Once more our Lord insists, "Just so, I tell you, there is joy before the angels of God over one sinner who repents" (Lk 15:10).

The third parable is the longest and most moving. A son gets his father to give him his inheritance, then leaves home and wastes it in evil living. When things go sour, he decides to return home so that he can eat. "I will go to my father and tell him: Father I no longer deserve to be called your son; treat me as one of your servants." This is hardly very noble, since his motive is hunger, but he does return. And here our Lord notes a wonderful detail which is the very heart of the parable: "But while he was yet at a distance, his father saw him and had compassion, and ran and embraced him and kissed him" (Lk 15:21). He doesn't even have time for his speech. As soon as he returns, he is accepted, not as a servant but as a son.

It's the same with God: he is always ready to forgive us and treat us as children returning to his friendship. In his mercy, he has established a special means—sacramental Confession—for us to express our repentance and be sure of his forgiveness. God wanted the Church to act on his behalf in forgiving sins through the mystery of the death of Christ. Jesus gave these powers to his apostles after his resurrection. "Receive the Holy Spirit. If you forgive the sins of any, they are forgiven; if you retain the sins of any, they are retained" (Jn 20:22–23). The Church ever since has forgiven sins in the name of Jesus Christ, in this way imitating what he did during his life on earth (cf. Mt 9:2).

By divine will, this sacrament is the ordinary means of returning from the death of sin to the life of grace. Although God works by grace as he wishes and could do things in another way—and does so if necessary—he wanted us to use this sacrament whenever we are conscious of having committed a grave sin, declaring the sin and our sorrow before a priest who absolves us in God's name if he finds us to be repentant.

In confessing one should say simply and clearly what grave sins one has committed: the kind of acts, their number, and any special circumstances that make them more grave (for example, it is ordinarily worse to insult a parent than a companion). It is not necessary to enter into unrelated details, such as one's name or the name of an accomplice, one's job, etc.

To encourage Catholics to use this sacrament, the Church many years ago set the obligation of confessing grave, or mortal, sins at least once a year, in the period of Easter. But grave sins should always be confessed before receiving Communion, whenever that occurs. Moreover, it is good to confess a serious sin as soon as possible in order to return to the life of grace. This should be done as often as required—twice a day if it comes to that—though without falling into scrupulosity.

Besides grave sins, Confession also is a place to ask God's forgiveness for all one's sins and faults. Venial or lesser sins do not cause the loss of the life of grace, but people who cherish their friendship with God usually feel the need of this sign of repentance. God undoubtedly is pleased by this, for it is one of the most obvious ways of growing in love for him. It is a good practice to confess venial sins and any failure in generosity toward God weekly or at least biweekly.

Repentance is central to living the Sacrament of Penance well. God does not require strong feelings of sorrow, because we are not always capable of them. It is enough to regret our sins and realize that they are offenses against God that damage our relationship with him. Repentance gives rise to the resolution to avoid falling again in the same way. Unless one is determined to do what one can to not offend God again, there is no true repentance. St. Francis de Sales cautions against "confessing venial sins out of mere habit, and conventionally, without making any effort to correct them" (*Introduction to the Devout Life*, II, 19).

After examination of conscience, sorrow, and resolutions comes the confession of sins to the confessor. This should be done with simplicity and briefly, while saying what is necessary and being complete. Superfluous remarks and speaking about others are to be avoided. Shame should not lead to silence or vagueness or distorting the truth about what is hardest to say. St. John of the Cross tells us not to prettify the ugly reality of sins, "which is more trying to excuse than to accuse" (*Dark Night*, 1, 2, 4). We are seeking God's forgiveness, not trying to look good to a priest. One should confess as if speaking face to face with Jesus himself.

"Beware of unmeaning self-accusations," says St. Francis de Sales. Among these he lists "I have not loved God as much as I ought"; "I have not prayed with as much devotion as I ought"; "I have not loved my neighbor as I ought"; "I have not received the sacraments with sufficient reverence"; and the like. "Such things as these are altogether useless in setting the state of your conscience before your confessor, inasmuch as all the saints in paradise and all men living would say the same" (*Introduction to the Devout Life*, II, 19). If one is going to mention insufficient devotion in prayer, specify that one was distracted by thinking of oneself; if it's not paying attention to someone, admit that you find him unpleasant. "Do not be content with saying that you told an untruth which injured no one; but say whether it was out of vanity, in order to win praise or avoid blame, out of heedlessness, or from obstinacy" (ibid.). It is also good to say whether these things happen often or infrequently.

Don't worry if you unintentionally forget something, even a mortal sin. Confess it the next time you receive the sacrament. To avoid scruples, don't make detailed lists of venial sins or write them down. It is enough to confess honestly what is remembered at that moment. If you need help, the priest can ask you questions. It also can be helpful to follow a certain order in confessing: the Ten Commandments, the capital sins, duties to God, neighbor, and to oneself, etc.

The final step in the confession is to do the particular penance the priest assigns. Ordinarily this is a prayer or some simple action; it is good to do it at once to avoid forgetting. Those prayers or actions have special value before God.

Frequent confession builds up interior life. It is a way to improve in the ascetical struggle and grow in love of God. It is important to choose a confessor well and become accustomed to confessing to him. In this way the confessor gets to know us and be more helpful to us even as our confessions improve. As a confessor one should seek a man who loves God, knows the ascetical life, is prudent and capable of making demands on us.

In this way, the confessor becomes a spiritual director. This is the term for someone who gives advice on how to grow in Christian life. His task is to give orientation, provide means, help one recognize God's will. A director does not act for us. He is like a friend who counsels loyally in regard to earthly loves. At times, the director may have to push a bit, but it is good that we be pushed to love God more.

A spiritual director is virtually indispensable to someone who wants to advance in this way. The saints have been unanimous on that. At times, God sheds extraordinary light on the paths of very simple souls, without giving it to those who can follow the ordinary path of Christian life. St. Vincent Ferrer wrote that God "never grants his grace to one who, having available a person capable of instructing and directing him, scorns this efficacious means of sanctification, thinking that he is self-sufficient and that he can by his own power, seek and find what is necessary for his salvation. . . . One who has a director and obeys him without reserve and in all things, will reach his goal much more easily and with greater speed than if he were alone, even though he himself might possess a more acute intellect and more wise books about spiritual things" (*De Vita Spirituali*, II, 1). A spiritual director can indicate the order one should follow in the ascent toward God, choose among possible resolutions, moderate excesses, overcome discouragement, encourage fortitude, resolve perplexities, point to the most apt means (readings, etc.).

How effective spiritual direction is depends to a great extent on the sincerity of the one directed. "Open your heart with all sincerity and faithfulness," urges St. Francis de Sales, "manifesting alike your good and your evil, without pretence or dissimulation" (*Introduction to the Devout Life*, 1, 4). It is not easy to disclose one's intimate life, especially if what is revealed is not flattering. Shame should not be an obstacle to sincerity. The reward is great, and this is a great way of defeating pride and vanity, which lie behind the resistance to looking bad. As the old saying goes, "be ashamed to sin"—but not to humbly confessing the sin.

It helps to bear in mind that people are very much alike. What happens to oneself has happened before to many others and will happen to many in the future. An experienced confessor has probably heard everything one could imagine and more. Hesitation to speak because we want his good opinion of us is clearly a manifestation of pride. That is one reason why one should not take evasive action like going to a confessor different from the usual one to confess something one is ashamed of. God rewards sincerity and is a friend of the humble; to conquer shame by telling what is humiliating is a first step that God will not fail to bless.

"'What shall I say? You asked when you began to open up your soul. And with a sure conscience, I answered: 'In the first place say what you would not like to be known'" (*Furrow*, no. 327). As pride decreases, peace and joy increase, since usually sorrow comes from too much self-love. "Your worries are at an end. You have discovered that being sincere with the director sorts out all complications with admirable ease" (*Furrow*, no. 335).

It is essential that the director speak to us clearly and that we listen to what he says. If we become sad or excuse ourselves as soon as he points out something that is not as it should be, we are not allowing ourselves to be directed. Where there are trust and affection, reproaches are more useful than empty praise. We know we are sinners: we should hardly be surprised if someone points this out in specific terms.

The spiritual director can give advice about a plan of life—practices of piety that help in living Christian life with greater intensity. He can recommend books as spiritual reading, and describe a way of practicing mental prayer (for example, how much time to spend and when to do it). He may counsel us about vocal prayers and assist us in improving our participation in the liturgy. Based on what he knows of us, he also can help us identify a particular examination of conscience: a specific point on which to concentrate the force of our interior struggle.

20.

Death and Life

In the third chapter of Genesis the first sin of mankind is described and the reason why sorrow and death entered the world is explained. God did not originally intend for the human race to experience those realities. "The wages of sin is death," says St. Paul (Rom 6:23).

Since then, suffering has been an inescapable part of life, and this continues until death. But sin and death have been transformed through the Cross of Christ. Christ, who had no sin, willed to taste pain and death, and converted them into the means of redemption. No longer is suffering only the penalty of sin: it is also its remedy.

United to the sacrifice of Christ on the Cross, suffering, pain, and our death acquire a purifying meaning. We can offer them, as did St. Paul, for our sins and those of all mankind: "Now I rejoice in my sufferings for your sake, and in my flesh I complete what is lacking in Christ's afflictions for the sake of his body, that is, the Church" (Col 1:24). Mysteriously but truly, we are "fellow heirs with Christ, provided we suffer with him in order that we may also be glorified with him" (Rom 8:17).

There is no avoiding suffering in this life. We are all too familiar with sickness and pain. And if we love greatly, we can count on many motives of sorrow. The egoist suffers only for himself, but one who wants to serve God and others will have suffering that comes to him from his loved ones and from the tasks he has undertaken for love of God. The more one loves, the more life gains in both joy and suffering.

Suffering often comes unexpectedly and brutally. The reaction must be Christian just the same. "At times the Cross appears without our looking for it: it is Christ who is seeking us out" (*The Way of the Cross*, Station 5). Do what is possible to avoid or remedy pain, then accept the will of God and unite yourself to Christ on the Cross. St. Paul is an example to us: "Afflicted in every way, but not crushed; perplexed, but not driven to despair; persecuted, but not forsaken; struck down, but not destroyed; always carrying in the body the death of Jesus, so that the life of Jesus may also be manifested in our bodies" (2 Cor 4:8–10).

But one should not exaggerate. Most pain is bearable. Even if it is great, one should not feel sorry for oneself. Forgetfulness of self is always best. "This is a characteristic of the just man," says St. Gregory the Great (seventh century), "that even in the midst of his sorrows and tribulations, he never neglects to concern himself about others" (*Moralia*, 3,9). "You said to me: Father, I am having a very rough time," wrote the Founder of Opus Dei. "In answer I whispered in your ear: Take upon your shoulders a small part of that cross, just a tiny part. And if you can't manage that then leave it entirely on the strong shoulders of Christ. And from this moment on, repeat with me: 'My Lord and my God: into your hands I abandon the past and the present and the future, what is small and what is great, what amounts to a little and what amounts to a lot, things temporal and things eternal.' Then, don't worry any more" (*The Way of the Cross*, Station 7).

People naturally prefer happiness and joy, but it is important to learn also to accept suffering with naturalness. Sorrow is only one more sign that we are on pilgrimage on this earth. "Here we have no lasting city, but we seek the city which is to come" (Heb 13:14).

And one day, when God wants it, we shall meet death. There is nothing extraordinary about death either. Many people have died and many more will. Still, it is repugnant to our nature. Accepting it is not easy; but without being anxious about it, a wise man or woman thinks about it often, accepting it, keeping it in mind, offering it to God, and placing themselves in his hands. The Church has the sacrament of the Anointing of the Sick to help us in the crisis of grave sicknesses and in preparation for death. Here is another way to increase, by grace, one's identification with the Passion and death of Christ.

Helpful, too, are words of St. Ignatius, Bishop of Antioch, already an old man when, in the year 107, he was taken to Rome to be thrown to the lions: "My love has been crucified, and there is no fire in me desiring to be fed; but there is within me a water that lives and speaks, saying to me inwardly, 'Come to the Father'" (*Letter to the Romans*, ch. 7).

Not only does our Lord expect us to accept suffering with joy and a Christian spirit, but he also desires that we seek the cross voluntarily. "If any man would come after me, let him deny himself and take up his cross and follow me. For whoever would save his life will lose it, and whoever loses his life for my sake will find it" (Mt 16:24–25). St. Augustine comments: "That cross which our Lord invites us to take up to follow him more quickly, what could it mean other than mortification?" (*Letter*, 243, 11).

Literally, to mortify something means to cause it to die. So to mortify oneself is, in a sense, to cause one's own death. St. Paul explains: "Put to death therefore what is earthly in you: fornication, impurity, passion, evil desire, and covetousness" (Col 3:6). One is to rid oneself of what belongs to the old man (cf. Eph 4:22; Col 3:4). And when the old man is part of oneself, that part must die: "For the desires of the flesh are against the Spirit" (Gal 5:17).

This takes place by mortifying passions or bad inclinations that are a consequence of original sin and personal sins; this is the aim of the ascetical struggle. Seen in the light of the love of God manifested in the sacrifice of the Cross, however, that struggle takes on new dimensions.

Love of God moves us to see in our weaknesses not only mistakes, but true sins that led to the death of Christ. We feel a desire to make reparation—to do penance, which means offering God sacrifices for our sins and the sins of others. John the Baptist and our Lord himself cried out: "Repent, for the kingdom of heaven is at hand" (Mt 3:2; 4:17). Mortification, voluntary sacrifice, is an unequivocal sign of love of God. St. Augustine says it "purifies, the soul, elevates the thoughts, subjugates the flesh itself to the spirit, makes the heart contrite and humble, dissipates the darkness of concupiscence, extinguishes the fire of the passions, and ignites the true light of chastity" (*Sermon*, 73).

Mortification should be a normal part of Christian life. Many people practice it for other reasons. "See how many sacrifices men and women make, willingly or less willingly, to take care of their bodies, protect their health, or gain the respect of others. . . . Are we unable to stir ourselves at the thought of the immensity of God's love, so poorly requited by men, and mortify what needs to be mortified so that our hearts and minds may be more attentive to Our Lord?" (*Friends of God*, no. 135).

The mortification most pleasing to God is that which helps us fulfill our obligations to God and to others. There are many opportunities for sacrifices in carrying out duties with perfection: following a schedule, being punctual, controlling the imagination in order to keep one's mind on what one is doing, not putting things off, finishing tasks well, and working or studying with intensity. Duties toward others also involve areas for mortification: helping those one lives with in their work or household tasks, smiling when one feels tired, doing what the others want instead of following one's own preferences in regard to recreation, visiting sick relatives or friends and those who are lonely, listening to those who feel a need to talk, etc.

Pride is a very important area for mortification. Since it is the most tenacious passion and the one hardest to defeat, many mortifications might well be directed at it: not thinking about oneself, not daydreaming about what one has done or might do, not speaking about oneself unless asked, not excusing oneself unless necessary, listening to others and not imposing one's opinion, not taking oneself too seriously or being offended by friendly kidding, not looking at oneself in the mirror more than necessary, etc.

The mortification of curiosity, the eagerness to know things that are not important, is very useful. It is relevant to a number of different contexts: in study, by centering our attention on what needs to be learned; in conversation, by avoiding gossip or criticism of others; in reading, by skipping material that is too easy or lacks cultural or human interest; in following the daily news, by avoiding scandalous or frivolous items.

Mortification is appropriate in choosing whom to associate with. Obviously there are some people we like more and have more to do with because of the ties of family, friendship, companionship, or gratitude. Otherwise, though—in school or the workplace or in an organization or group—one needn't be guided simply by likes and dislikes. Yes, some people are more likable than others, often for superficial reasons like looks, but that shouldn't be grounds for giving them preferential treatment, which is unjust and at times offensive. It's a good rule to treat those one likes least just as one treats those one likes better.

There are opportunities for mortification in regard to detachment. At times, one can, and even should, resist buying something, or postpone that, because it isn't necessary. One can refrain from using something good for a few days or in some circumstances (e.g., take public transportation instead of the car, skip TV and read a book or have a conversation). It's a good mortification to give away little objects to which one has become attached: pens, figurines, souvenirs, emblems, etc.

Mortification in eating and drinking is a necessity. "The day you leave the table without having done some small mortification you have eaten like a pagan" (*The Way*, no. 681). More than not eating, this means offering God something: eating or drinking a little less (one glass of wine instead of two), not complaining about the food, eating something one doesn't like, not having seconds or dessert, delaying drinking, not buttering the bread, not using gravy, not starting to eat until everyone has been served (which is also a rule of good manners), not eating between meals, not drinking hard liquor, or certain types of liquor, etc. One needn't do all these mortifications all the time or the same ones constantly. Ingenuity and love of God are the guide here.

Corporal mortifications are sacrifices offered to God by mortifying tendencies of the body. Here, as everywhere else, moderation is required: we shouldn't damage our health. "By abstinence we have to extinguish the vices of the flesh, not the flesh," says St. Gregory the Great (*Moralia*, 20, 41, 78). But the opposite extreme should also be avoided. Being too easy on themselves weakens people; being a bit demanding and austere is one of the best guarantees of long life. Athletes are testimony to the fact that the effort, fatigue, and pain it takes to perform will also—if done with moderation—improve health. St. Paul cites them as an example: "Every athlete exercises self-control in all things. They do it to receive a perishable wreath, but we an imperishable." (1 Cor 9:25).

A number of things fall under the heading of mortifying the body. Posture is one. You can offer up not sinking in an armchair, taking rather a harder or less comfortable seat, trying to sit erect, not crossing your legs. Then there is sleep. Sleep is necessary, and seven or eight hours a night are usually about right. But it's an excellent mortification to rise punctually when the alarm goes off, instead of grabbing a few more minutes in bed (which always leads to disorders like lateness or sloppy dress). Also part of it is going to bed on time instead of wasting time on trivia. Sleeping on a hard bed can be a mortification, and saints have found it a healthy one. Or one can try not using a pillow. But whatever you do, be sure to get a good night's sleep, since God expects a good day's work from you tomorrow.

Taking a cold (or cool) shower is another good mortification that makes us stronger by submitting the body to the discipline of the spirit and offers a sacrifice to God. Referring to the fact that within the Mystical Body of Christ, the Church, we are Christ's "members," St. Bernard exclaimed, "Weak members should be ashamed of being under a head crowned with thorns" (*Sermon*, 5; *on the feast of All Saints*, 9).

The practice of fasting has a long and distinguished history. Starting in the third century and continuing well into the Middle Ages, Christians fasted twice a week, eating only after sunset. Special times of fasting were also observed, including Advent and especially Lent. Today there are reminders in the fasts the Church prescribes for Ash Wednesday and Good Friday, when people eat only one full meal and a small amount at breakfast and lunch.

There are many other corporal mortifications in the Christian tradition. St. Thomas More wore a hair shirt as penance under his robes as Chancellor of England. St. Dominic and St.

Francis of Assisi used disciplines (small whips), and the rules of monastic orders and congregations prescribed the use of cilices. They were used by St. Teresa and St. John of the Cross and by many other religious and lay people. Note, though, that the saints always recommended moderation in such matters. No one should undertake strange or severe penance without consulting his or her spiritual director.

The penance God asks of us has to take shape in the countless small details that improve our service to others and our dedication to God. We need to take seriously our Lord's words: "Unless a grain of wheat falls into the earth and dies, it remains alone; but if it dies, it bears much fruit" (Jn 12:24); "If any man would come after me, let him deny himself and take up his cross daily and follow me" (Lk 9:23).

21.

Love for the Church

The sacrifice of Christ led to a new Covenant sealed with his blood (cf. 1 Cor 11:25; Lk 22:20; Heb 9:15) and constituted a new people of God, a new worship, and a new priesthood. This new pact had been predicted by Jeremiah for the Messianic times: "I will put my law within them, and I will write it upon their hearts; and I will be their God, and they shall be my people" (Jer 31:33; Heb 8:10).

Men were incorporated into the old Israel through the rite of circumcision, which made them participators in God's Covenant with his people. One is incorporated into the new People of God by receiving the Holy Spirit, ordinarily through the sacraments (cf. Rom 2:28; Col 2:11; Phil 3:2). When God's grace is within us—as it is as long as we are free of grave sin—we are living members of the new People of God, the Church. The Holy Spirit is, as it were, the seal authenticating our legitimacy as heirs of the definitive promise of the Kingdom of God into which we shall one day enter as God's children. The Holy Spirit, who makes us children of God with what might be called a family resemblance to Christ, is the sign that we are "a chosen race, a royal priesthood, a holy nation, God's own people" (1 Pet 2:9). The Holy Spirit is thus the cause of our unity in the Church.

The Church therefore is much more than an assembly of believers, like a human association or society established by its members' decision to unite. The Church is a sacred institution, founded by Jesus Christ, whose life depends on the indwelling of the Holy Spirit in each of its members. The Spirit is the ultimate explanation of the life of faith and of hope. It is the beginning of what will be, at the end of time, the Kingdom of Heaven, uniting all its members, not only those who are living but those who have died and already enjoy the intimate life of God in heaven; indeed, all those men and women, including those not juridically members of the Church and even those not baptized, into whose hearts God has poured his Spirit. The bonds uniting the Church are thus much deeper and more profound than those uniting a visible human society. This mysterious reality is commonly expressed by saying that the Holy Spirit is the "soul" of the Church.

St. Paul expresses the unity of Christians in Christ by the image of a body: "For just as the body is one and has many members, and all the members of the body, though many, are one body, so it is with Christ. For by one Spirit we were all baptized into one body" (1 Cor 12:12–13). Christ is the head (Eph 5:25), that is, the one who gives unity to the body; we are the members, who live the very life of Christ (cf. Col 1:18; Eph 1:23; Col 2:17).

The Church is the instrument God wills to spread salvation among men, and by incorporating ourselves in it, we participate in the redemption worked by Christ. Through the Church, we receive Christ's teaching. In the Church, we are baptized, participate in the Eucharistic sacrifice and receive Communion, and have our sins forgiven.

God desires that we come to him through the Church. Thus Christian life does not grow in isolation but within the bosom of this new People. Nor can we separate our relationship with God from the life of the Church, for the Holy Spirit acting in our souls is the same Person who sustains the life of the Church.

Christ intended that there be diverse functions within the Church. Not all were called apostles, but "he appointed twelve, to be with him, and to be sent out to preach and have authority to cast out demons" (Mk 3:14–15). To these, after his resurrection, he gave the power of forgiving sins (cf. Jn 20:33) and the mission of preaching throughout the world (Mt 28:19–20). They were "ministers of a new covenant" (2 Cor 3:6) whose task was to celebrate the Eucharist in memory of the Lord and speak in his name.

Among the apostles, Jesus singled out Simon, whose name he changed to Peter, thus pointing to a new mission given by God. "Cephas" in Aramaic or "Petros" in Greek signified "rock." Although it was not used as a proper name, Christ gave it to this apostle to signify that he was to be the foundation on which he would build his Church (Mt 16:18–19).

Peter—and after him his successors, the popes—received the mission of governing the flock of Christ and confirming all its members in the faith. The pope is the vicar or representative of Christ on earth, whose mission is to maintain the unity of the Church. The unity of each member with Christ finds expression in unity with the pope. This is what is meant by saying one is "in communion" with him, sharing the same faith and moral truths, and using the same means of salvation, the sacraments, instituted by Jesus.

The bishops, who are the successors of the apostles, have a similar mission in the local churches. Catholics should be in communion with their bishop and he with the pope. For a bishop, as for all other Catholics, communion with the pope means communion with the universal Church. Within his own jurisdiction, each bishop has the duty of safeguarding unity of doctrine, spreading it by preaching, and administering the sacraments to the faithful. In that mission priests and deacons are his collaborators.

The pope, bishops, priests, and deacons make up the hierarchy and form the governing body of the Church. But this government is not the same as that of a civil society. This is so fundamentally because one becomes part of the hierarchy by means of a sacrament, Holy Orders, which empowers the recipient to exercise the diaconate, priesthood, or episcopate. Without it, one cannot ordain priests (in the case of bishops) and forgive sins and celebrate the Eucharist (in the case of priests).

The basic mission of the hierarchy is to preach the truths of faith and morality and to administer the sacraments. The essentials cannot change. Priests can explain doctrine and the sacraments, but they cannot change them. Outside these specified areas, the hierarchy does not intervene in the lives of Catholics. It provides moral criteria or rules of behavior, but does not pronounce on the technical aspects of economic, political, or medical questions.

The Church as a whole and those who govern it are assisted by the Holy Spirit to discover and apply the contents of faith and morality. He guarantees the authenticity of preaching and sees to it that the deposit of truth that the Church possesses is not lost. He assists those who have the public function of teaching the truth of Christ so that their preaching is without error. The Church holds that there cannot be error in doctrine believed for centuries, proposed with moral unanimity as a serious matter bearing upon salvation by the bishops throughout the world in union with the pope or joined with him in an ecumenical council, or simply proclaimed by the pope as supreme pastor of the Church with the intention of defining it as part of the faith. The infallibility of the Church is expressed in all these modes of teaching.

Obviously, since the hierarchy is made up of men of flesh and blood, they will have defects. The apostles had them—all of them abandoned Christ on the Cross and Peter denied him three times—and so do all of us have them. But a Catholic should distinguish between human defects and sacred functions. We honor deacons, priests, bishops, and the pope not for what they are as men, but insofar as they represent Jesus Christ, and we love them because we love Christ. It harms the unity of the Church to speak badly of them.

The Church through the centuries has done a vast amount of good. The action of the Holy Spirit has transformed millions of men and women and called forth countless heroic examples of service to others and love of God. Millions have devoted their lives to serving the sick, the dying, the aged, educating children and young people, and spreading Christian doctrine, and these things have been done through the many institutions of the Church. Even more millions of Catholics have lived exemplary family lives, cared for their needy and sick, given an example of honesty in business, industry, agriculture, and public life. The biographies of the saints comprise only one chapter in a far larger volume.

The Church has also been the impetus of a huge civilizing effort to which Western culture owes its very existence. Among the results are innumerable expressions of Christian art, which form the richest and most abundant artistic patrimony of the human race.

In modern times, nevertheless, people who do not like the Church have sought to obliterate the memory of all this, while emphasizing and often manipulating negative episodes. It is true of course that people usually have the mindset and defects of their particular time and place along with their personal weaknesses. The surprising thing, however, is that love of God enabled so many to rise above the faults of their own time as well as those common to people at all times. The conclusion is clear: "A man cannot act in accordance with his Christian faith, cannot truly believe in the Holy Spirit, unless he loves the Church and trusts it. He cannot be a consistent Christian if he limits himself to pointing out the deficiencies and limitations of some who represent the Church, judging her from the outside, as though he were not her son" (*Christ Is Passing By*, no. 130).

It is typical of God's way of acting in history that the Church is humanly rather weak. Christ was born as a helpless infant in a village stable and died humiliated by men by a form of execution often reserved to slaves. God prefers to be present among us without making a great show, perhaps so that our love for him is completely free. The Church shares in that weakness. It has been shaken by the winds of history, and one of the clearest evidences of its divinity is that it has not succumbed. Sometimes it has been persecuted, other times powerful people have used it for personal gain. In the present as well as in the past the Church has encountered totalitarian systems unable to tolerate an institution proclaiming without compromise the truth that comes from God. And from the time of Herod until now it has suffered at the hands of those who resent Christian morality as a judgment on their own conduct.

Since the seventeenth century a certain current of thought has been engaged in the project of creating a new humanity without morality by spreading a negative image of the Church. This involves unjustly associating it with backwardness, obscurantism, superstition, and anti-scientific thinking. It is an element in the persecution of the Church that is going on now.

The Church has always faced difficulties. Christ himself said that in his field—the "field" of history—wheat and weeds would grow together (cf. Mt 13:24–30). The Church has seen Satan's hand in the succession of persecutions, often strange ones with a strong irrational component. Christ foresaw all this (cf. Lk 22:31), but he promised Peter that "the powers of death shall not prevail" against the Church (Mt 16:18). The Holy Spirit is at its heart. Christ will never abandon it (cf. Mt 28:20). Speaking of the boat of which we read in the gospel, fragile and tossed about by the waves and wind of that Sea of Galilee, St. Augustine says: "There traveled in it not only the disciples, but Christ himself. Therefore, do not leave the ship and pray to God. When all of the means seem to fail, when the rudder doesn't function, and the torn sails turn into a greater danger, when one has lost all hope of human assistance, think that all that remains is to pray to God. He, who ordinarily brings sailors happily to port, should not abandon the barque of the Church" (*Sermon*, 63:4).

The worst danger, because it is most harmful, is not from outside but from within. Persecution strengthens the Church while the infidelity of its members weakens it. A Christian has the grave responsibility of living a holy life. "Not in itself," points out St. Ambrose, "but in us, its living members, does the Church receive wounds, and therefore we have to try not to afflict her with our falls" (*Treatise on Virginity*, 48). But our fidelity also affects the Church for the better. This mysterious unity is called the communion of saints.

Unity is the greatest good of the Church. Christ prayed "that all may be one" at the Last Supper (Jn 17:22), and we must do all we can to promote it. The unity of the Church begins with the life of the Holy Spirit in everyone living in grace. It is expressed visibly in communion with the Roman Pontiff, in loving and praying for him and readily receiving teaching, in love for all the bishops, especially the bishop of one's own diocese, praying for him and obeying him. It finds expression also in the common goods of the whole Church—the truths of faith and morality and the sacraments—which we seek to share with others. Love for the unity of the Church means, finally, having a heart that reaches out to embrace all Christians. "If you want to love Christ," St. Augustine says, "extend your love to the whole world, because the members of Christ are all over the world" (*Commentary on the First Epistle of St. John*, 10, 5).

22.

Mary, the Mother of God

St. Paul begins his explanation of the Incarnation of God's Word: "When the plenitude of times arrived, God sent his Son, born of a woman" (Gal 4:4). At this central moment of history, when the divine was closest to the human, God sent an angel to ask for the collaboration of a young woman, almost a child, living in a village in a remote corner of Israel (Lk 1:26–27).

God did not consult rulers or priests or learned men or any political or doctrinal authority. He did seek the collaboration of a young girl of Nazareth. God does not operate according to human logic. "'For my thoughts are not your thoughts, neither are your ways my ways,' says the Lord. 'For as the heavens are higher than the earth, so are my ways higher than your ways and my thoughts than your thoughts'" (Is 55:8–9).

The young woman was to be the Mother of God. But first God explained what was to happen within her and waited on her consent. Then she showed her complete availability for what God wanted: "Behold, I am the handmaid of the Lord; let it be to me according to your word" (Lk 1:31–38).

Mary's unconditional yes to God manifests the greatness of her soul. God had prepared her to be his Mother, and the mysterious words of the angel's greeting speak of a singular quality: "Hail Mary, full of grace, the Lord is with you."

We learn even more about her from events a short time later in the home of Elizabeth, her cousin, who the angel had told her was soon to have a son. The charity of the Blessed Virgin and her enthusiasm for the message received led her—quickly, the evangelist says—to that house so many miles away. There she received a marvelous greeting from Elizabeth: "Blessed are you among women and blessed is the fruit of your womb! And why is this granted me, that the mother of my Lord should come to me? For behold, when the voice of your greeting came to my ears, the babe in my womb leaped for joy. And blessed is she who believed that there would be a fulfillment of what was spoken to her from the Lord."

Elizabeth's praise joins with the immense joy Mary bore in her soul to produce the exaltation of the Magnificat in which our Lady declares her understanding of the logic of God: "My soul magnifies the Lord, and my spirit rejoices in God my Savior, for he has regarded the low estate of his handmaiden. For behold, henceforth all generations will call me blessed; for he who is mighty has done great things for me" (Lk 1:42–49).

Truly Mary is blessed among all women—not through her merits, but through the great things done in her by the All-Powerful. She is God's servant for whatever he wants of her. She knows that what God loves in her, above all, is her humility—the humility proper to one who knows herself to be, next to God, nothing—a slave.

With this instrument, Mary, God initiated the redemption of the world. God did not seek power, or learning; he sought humility, love, and dedication, freely given. All those who were close to Christ in his early years were humble people living ordinary lives who gave themselves freely to God.

God had no need of human means in order to redeem, but he made use of those he chose to use and especially of that heartfelt commitment that is all he really seems to look for in humankind. Mary's cooperation in God's plans is, very much like what another woman might have done: simply to give birth to Christ, nurture him, care for him for years, while devoting most of her life to the domestic tasks of a woman living in a village of that time and place. Her days were filled with ordinary work, often difficult and always done with much love. What gave her life extraordinary value was the love of God. That is God's logic and the message of Mary.

"If God exalted his Mother," the founder of Opus Dei said, "it is equally true that he did not spare her pain, exhaustion in her work, or trials of her faith." What was proper to Mary was the living out of her *fiat*, "sincerely, unstintingly, fulfilling its every consequence, but never amid fanfare, rather in the hidden and silent sacrifice of each day." Here was the contribution God expected from her to the redemption of mankind. "As we meditate on these truths, we come to understand better the logic of God. We come to realize that the supernatural value of our life does not depend on accomplishing great undertakings suggested to us by our overactive imagination. Rather it is to be found in the faithful acceptance of God's will, in welcoming generously the opportunities for small, daily sacrifice" (*Christ Is Passing By*, no. 172).

If serving God required doing great things, few would measure up, and then only by some accident of birth or external circumstances. Most people would have hardly any part in God's plans. But the redemption was carried out in the midst of what was ordinary and hidden. The greater part of the lives of our Lord and Mary and Joseph was spent in this way. "All of us are called to share the kingdom of heaven—each with his own vocation: in his home, his work, his civic duties and the exercise of his rights" (*Christ Is Passing By*, no. 44).

All men and women are called by God to collaborate in redemption through silent, hidden sacrifice. Most likely, this is what God intends for you and me. And even if there were something remarkable about our lives, we would soon enough find in them what is normal, everyday, simple, and humble. This is where we must learn to love God.

True, in accomplishing the redemption God made use of the genius of St. Paul, the strength of St. Peter, the courage and influence of Joseph of Arimathea (Mk 15:43). He continues to use the wisdom, wealth, good name, and talent of men and women in carrying out his plans. But these are merely starting points for their service, and people who have them must learn to think of them this way. They are responsibilities, "talents" to be used for God and others.

That is not easy. Pride often turns motives for service into motives for vanity. Talents are frequently placed at the service of egoism. Here is the meaning of those words of our Lord that sounded so harsh to his disciples: "It will be hard for a rich man to enter the kingdom of heaven" (Mt 19:23). God will require an accounting from us for the use we make of the talents we receive.

Mary was called to show her love in hidden and silent sacrifice. But God depended on her far more than on any other human being. Now, too, in the work of redemption he uses resources that escape our notice: prayer, suffering, the small sacrifices and penances of sick people, mothers, the elderly, workers, peasants, cloistered religious, and so many others who receive little or no attention from the world.

In the life of grace there is a vast area that is not seen. What does Christ's life have to do with ours? Yet we know by faith that grace—the Holy Spirit acting in our souls—is transforming us into Christ, and that this comes about through his Passion and death. How can the prayer and sacrifice of men and women who unite themselves to the prayer and sacrifice of Christ affect us? Yet God wants many good things to come about in that way.

In the world that is visible only to the eyes of faith, Mary occupies a very special place. Consider the last words of Christ crucified: "But standing by the cross of Jesus were his mother, and his mother's sister, Mary the wife of Clopas, and Mary Magdalene. When Jesus saw his mother, and the disciple whom he loved standing near, he said to his mother, 'Woman, behold, your son!' Then he said to the disciple, 'Behold, your mother!' And from that hour the disciple took her to his own home" (Jn 19:25–27). John was the only disciple present at the foot of the cross. He received Mary as his mother. And so all receive her who desire to be faithful followers of Christ. As Origen says: "Really, anyone who has identified with Christ no longer lives for him or herself, but Christ lives in him, and given that he lives in Christ, Jesus said of him to Mary, Behold your son: Christ" (*On the Gospel of St. John*, 19, 26). She is the mother of every Christian who identifies with her son.

Therefore she is also the Mother of the Church, the Mystical Body of Christ, as she was—though in a different way—of his physical body. "By her charity," says St. Augustine, "she cooperated in having the faithful born in the Church, members of that Head of whom she was the true mother physically" (*De Virginitate*, 6). Pope Paul VI honored her officially with this title, Mother of the Church.

Mary was present at the first steps taken by that Church after the resurrection, and undoubtedly she played a role in fostering unity and strength in the faith (cf. Acts 1:14). The Church since then has always grown close to Mary, manifesting its devotion to her throughout the centuries. Love for Jesus leads one to love all that he loved, above all his mother.

The Church sees in Mary an intercessor before God. She shows us his benevolent face, brings us closer to him, helps us to discover Christ. Devotion to Mary is focused on Christ, the one mediator between God and man, and her action in the Church is essentially to repeat what she told the servants at the wedding feast in Cana: "Do whatever he tells you" (Jn 2:5).

There are times when we feel unable—unworthy—to deal with God face to face. Mary is there to help us, encouraging us to be filled with the spirit of prayer. Thinking of her, we learn to live in a Christian way. Contemplating her, we learn to love God. Prayer to Mary is already an imitation of her life. To her is entrusted, in a special way, the holiness of our loving.

Marian devotions are delightfully simple. The most popular, the Rosary, consists mainly of the repetition of two prayers: the Hail Mary and the Our Father. Yet, simple as this is, there is nothing more profound than to contemplate the mysteries of our redemption, allowing them to sink deeply into our minds and hearts.

Whoever considers the Rosary too simple for him has not understood God's logic. Neither has he understood the value of Mary's life of hidden and silent sacrifice and the lives of the vast majority of human beings—ordinary lives filled with joy, suffering, struggle, and love. He may imagine that God is better served by showy activity. But we do not serve God by serving our own tastes. God uses our talents when we dedicate them to him, not when we attempt to do as we prefer. The simple piety of the Rosary and other Marian devotions is especially necessary for those whose pride in their gifts might tempt them to stray from the path that leads to God.

"Unless you turn and become like children, you will never enter the kingdom of heaven" (Mt 18:3). One who learns to deal with Mary as with his mother will feel like a child before God, and he who is mighty will do great things for him just as he did for her (cf. Lk 1:49). Trusting conversation with Mary introduces us to this intimacy with God.

And here is the aim of the whole Christian life. This book has tried to explain how it can be reached. One means God uses to help us on the way is devotion to Mary. With reason, it has been said that she is like a short cut for living the interior life. Thus we conclude with words of an old hymn:

Vitam praesta puram	Bestow a pure life,
iter para tutum	Prepare a safe way:
ut videntes Jesum	That seeing Jesus,
semper collaetemur. Amen.	We may ever rejoice. Amen.

—*Ave Maris Stella*